MY DISQUIET GENE

SHARING MYSELF

*I believe someone
sprayed the family
tree and I was spared
the torment of genius*

BY

JERRY HEINTZBERGER

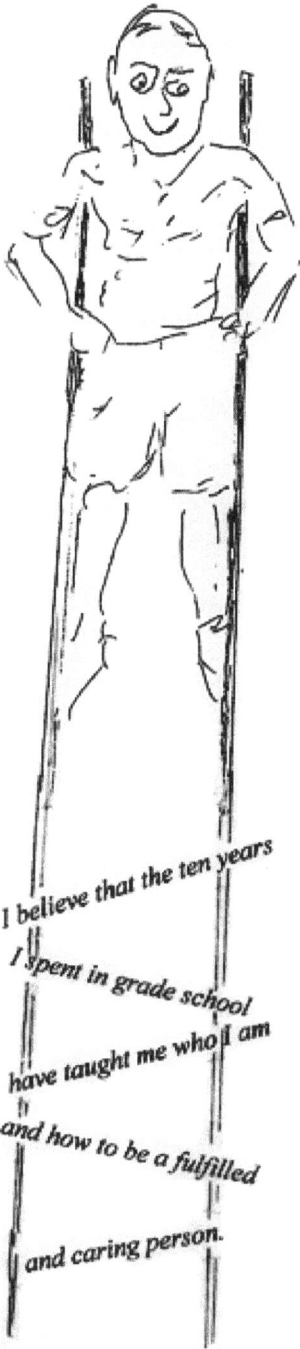

I believe that the ten years
I spent in grade school
have taught me who I am
and how to be a fulfilled
and caring person.

Published in 2011 by
Ashgrey Publishing Company
Palm Springs CA and Lausanne, Switerland

Printed in the United States of America

Prologue

My Disquiet Gene is appropriately titled as it completes my story that I wish to share. Hopefully, it can contribute to research in some way. The original incomplete manuscript was titled, *The Essence of Early Childhood*.

San Diego 1984
Jerry, 57 years old; Henry 69 years old

This writing began as a therapeutic exercise after having read the autobiography of my oldest brother where he gave praise to the teachers in the parochial elementary school that we both attended. Unlike Henry who was an academic trail blazer and model pupil, I had attention deficit, was a failure and endured humiliating experiences. This journal helped me put in perspective some of the dynamic trends and social fabric of the times. I developed an awareness that all life fluctuates in accordance with the propelling force behind evolution.

At an early age I began to understand myself, the makeup of some of my genes, my sexuality, and the grass roots whence I came. Given my "disquiet gene" and circumstances as stated, my life choices were in sync, as I have come to believe, with planet earth's physiological state/times. This writing blends the many forces that formed my character, my acceptance/rejection, my values and the paths that some loved ones have traveled. I conclude with an optimistic view for planet earth, but not without expressing concern for my ten percent of the population and my dishonor for the Vatican.

There is focus on the uncompromising dogma of the Catholic Church during my early years and my current concern with our overly populated planet. There is speculation as to what ends religion can disrupt, blind and destroy.

One liners and specific quotations are included that amplify my narration. Many are humorous, some sober, and the grave quotations do reflect my serious outlook. They were found in E. C. McKenzie's 1400 Quips and Quotes; The Home Book of American Quotations, by Bruce Bohle, and The Book of Positive Quotations, by John Cook. Tidbits of history from the Internet Accounting.

1

Of all my memoirs that I might share,
I'll admit to my crippling despair.
 Of learning reading when I was young,
 A failure was I, learning a foreign tongue.

I was just a tad of six or seven,
Grouped with as many as four times eleven.
 While some learned to decipher each line as they read.
 For me each line was a blurb in my head.

It wasn't just reading that I longed for a fix en,
I longed for a change from those righteous mean vixen.
 Whatever it was we did not relate,
 They were more than I could equilibrate.

Ten long years I had to endure
As voted the boy with the most failure.
 To be more me I unshackled my mind.
 Knowledge, emotion and desire were prime.

My dreams were that I'd be as good as the rest,
When compared to those who shared my nest.
 I enrolled in an art school way out West,
 To increase my talents as I knew best.

New faces and places were unfamiliar,
But I didn't feel the least peculiar.
 I pushed a broom to earn my fare,
 And I was a happy debonair.

A doctor, a painter who was an internist,
Soon became my psychoanalyst.
 Dyslexics like me, he did surmise,
 Are not likely to win a Nobel Prize.
A tutor for me he did find.
Someone who can fix my mind.
 Once I got the fine points of read and write,
 I was no longer a parasite.

Reading and writing became my mainstay.
Life unfolded like a miracle play,
 My autobiography tells the whole story,
 Its not salacious, its not boring,

I just may be the new valedictory.

Ode

to

Reading

Religion

I grew up with Jerry and have spent my

entire life at his side.

Jerry has much disdain for matters

of religious righteousness as demonstrated

in his years in parochial school.

The telling of his story exemplifies,

in part, the righteous, zealous, moralizing

that can do much to thwart spiritual growth.

In today's world, with shrinking borders,

there should be no place for the likes of

such preaching, as:

"The one and only true religion"

Profits generated

from this autobiography,

My Disquiet Gene,

will go to the

Gerald Heintzberger

Early Childhood Fund

Administered by a

San Diego Foundation

Contents

Dedication

I dedicate this to my parents

Catherine Sofia Heintzberger
1889 – 1967

Henry John Heintzberger
1882 – 1942

to my mentor

Dr. Robert Helm Kennicott
1892 – 1983

My gratitude to

Friend Mike Nissen, who, sixty years ago,
was an influence for my choosing the teaching profession
and with our daily phone chats has encouraged me to
publish this autobiography

Early Photographs

Pop 1914   *Mom 1914*

Photo September 1923

Mother 7-30-1889   Father 9-13-1882

Henry 12-24-1915 Catherine 9-26-1918 Alberta 2-21-1917
William 1-28-1921 Baby Herman 1-16-1923

Not born: Charles 6-29-1924 Gerald 9-10-27

Introduction: Brother Henry's Account of His Grammar School Days

"The classrooms were quite large and our classes usually had from 50 to 55 pupils." "In order to compensate for the class size, discipline was quite strict and the nuns tolerated no horseplay." "One nun handled the entire class and the same nun taught all the subjects." "These subjects included penmanship, reading, grammar, arithmetic, history, geography and religious studies." "These nuns were a very dedicated group and the fact was that, in spite of all the odds, they still did an excellent job of teaching as indicated by the fact that many of us from the parochial schools became honor students in the public high school. In 1934 I was named valedictorian of a class of 221 students at Mishawaka High School and the 1935 valedictorian also came from Saint Joseph's school. It was not long after we moved to Mishawaka that Herman was born in 1923, Charles in 1924 and Gerald in 1927. Each of the children as they grew followed in the same path through Saint Joseph's School and the Mishawaka High School." "They were happy years for all of us."

Mishawaka - rear yard
Henry & Jerry Circa 1935

 Henry wrote his autobiography after he celebrated his eightieth birthday. There is a twelve year age difference and I received a copy of his working manuscript after I had my eightieth birthday. In 1999 Henry sent a draft to our brother Herman. Herman didn't reply and died shortly thereafter. When closing her father's belongings, daughter Nancy stored the likes of such papers. A few years later she discovered them, and thus, I received a copy in November 2007.

Henry
Hank

Alberta
Berta

Catherine
Kate

William
Bill

Etched Memories

Herman
Herm

I was born September 10, 1927, twelve years after my oldest Brother, Henry. Those years and the following years reflect many changes within the dynamics of the family, the social fabric of the times and particularly the formable school years as Henry experienced them.

Aside from the time spent in the classrooms at Saint Joseph School, my childhood would have been extremely happy. My impressionable years of family life were most prominent between the ages of four, 1931, through 1936, at age nine. I can vividly recall the resonance of voices coming from the seating at that round dining table in our home. Mom and Pop and we siblings created a united family of kindred spirits where each had a voice to speak. Pop sat at the head of the table with Henry, the oldest and his namesake, on his right, Alberta, the oldest daughter on his left. Mom sat at the opposite end with me, the youngest on her right and Chuck on her left. I remember the laughter that was interspersed with discussion, especially at meals end. Pop and Mom made frequent references to life in the "old country." Henry, Alberta and Kate were most compatible with references to new board or card games and books. Bill always had much to contribute. His yarn often related to singing in the church choir and what Mr. Kunkel, the director, had to say. My recollection of Herman at that time was his complacency to process all that was being said. In time, his forte was in scouting and his enthusiasm for sports shown later. Chuck was the individual who always provided leverage to any talk as his humor was woven into all subject matter. Yep, I had the essence of good home schooling!

Charles
Chuck

Gerald
Jerry

15

In The Beginning – the Formative Years

My mother, Sofia Catherine Van Amersfoort Heintzberger was born in Arnhem, Holland on July 30, 1889. She was the oldest of seven siblings. My father, Henry John Heintzberger was born September 13, 1882 in Doesburg, Holland. I believe my father was the third oldest of thirteen children. Mom's parents were in the cigar manufacturing business that thrived for several centuries. Pop's father is reported to have been an extremely thrifty man who worked diligently to establish the Doesburg Candy Factory.

My parents didn't immigrate to the U. S. together. Mom had been engaged to another man who had an untimely death from pneumonia. Pop had a girl friend in Holland who might have joined him but she entertained fears of going to a primitive environment and broke off the relationship. Mom came to the U.S. on the Holland American Line, the Rotterdam in 1912, the same year that the Titanic sailed. Pop came as the clouds of World War One were gathering in Europe. Pop's friend, Brother Willibrord, a religious at the University of Notre Dame in South Bend, Indiana, offered Pop a job as baker at the university. Pop emigrated without hesitation. He had a job waiting for him so he didn't have to go through Ellis Island in New York.

Site of the ancestral candy factory

Pop's formal schooling was complete after five years at which time, age eleven, he was apprentice to a baker to learn the trade. From age eleven, 1893 to 1912, he traveled by bicycle throughout that country and earned the title, "Master Baker." He worked in a wide variety of bakeries in that small country, 190 miles long and about 160 miles wide.

When my parents met, Mom had employment as a nanny in South Bend. They married on Valentine's Day, 1915. While they had a mortgage on the house they bought, Pop proudly talked about paying cash for all of the household furnishings. Their honeymoon house has since been torn down and the site is now part of Notre Dame's campus.

Pop and Mom enjoyed reminiscing about the happy times in the "Old Country," with the beauty of the canals, the bicycle paths, the gardens and the manicured homes that they left behind. Pop enjoyed describing the architecture of the edifice where he was born. The basement had balusters that supported the three stories above. One baluster had the date inscribed on it regarding repair work that was attended to. If I recall correctly the date was before 1600. Homes

Gera Verheek Heintzberger
1857 - 1930

Johannes HendrikusHeintzberger
1854 - 1931

back then were taxed according to the number of rooms in them, so closets were eliminated and armoires were used. Pop's entire family slept in trundle beds built into the walls.

January 1990 I visited the area that was both home and candy factory where Pop was born and spent his formative years. The front of the building has been converted to a dry goods store and there are apartments throughout. It is located on a street that is not as wide as present day planners would have, but picturesque with window awnings and flower boxes. It is directly across from a large stone Catholic Church that struck me as interesting since Holland is a Protestant country. Pop's mother was Protestant and converted to Catholicism when she married.

There were occasions before the United States entered World War II when Mom and Pop mailed food packages to Pop's sister, as Holland was occupied by Nazis. Pop kept close contact with siblings, especially his sister, Joanna. In all her photos Aunt Joanna was wearing dresses with long sleeves. Pop felt somewhat responsible for her being disfigured ever since they were youngsters. They were playing and running when he and a brother ran her into the candy factory's kitchen where she inadvertently tilted a kettle of boiling sugar that spilled onto her. I faintly recall some of the correspondence between Pop and his siblings in 1932, to settle the estate after grandfather died. The siblings were interested in deeding the real estate proceeds to Aunt Joanna for her retirement as she had remained a spinster.

Mom was raised by her grandparents. The city, Amersfoort, was named after her ancestors. Mom kept a box of her family photos that I enjoyed viewing. The photo of her grandparents celebrating their golden wedding anniversary with fancy head dress appears most festive. Mom's photo in her first communion dress, or confirmation dress and veil, appear extravagant compared with today's rituals. Thirty some years after Mom left

Mom's Grandparents' Golden Wedding - Holland

her home in Arnhem, her eighteen year old son, Charles, was wounded in that city near her home during World War Two's lethal Battle of the Bulge.

Mother

My parents believed it was important for their children that they be assimilated into the culture of their new country. English was always spoken. In those days there was a stigma if a foreign language was spoken in the home. We siblings learned only a few Dutch words like "fadaduke" for dishcloth and "stuff and blick" for dustpan and small broom. Both parents had Dutch accents but Mom's was more pronounced than Pop's as he encountered more people outside the home. Mom's accent was such that my name, Jerry, came out as Sherry. All seven of us siblings received genuine loving care from both parents. Kate's reminiscence often recalled the loving care that Pop and Mom gave to her at age two when she was recovering from polio and her legs required frequent bathing. Pop never laid a hand on any of us. Mom was the designator person for spankings and I did warrant a few. I believe all siblings had a strong streak of individuality. Our parents were good at directing and encouraging without undo criticism or control.

What I remember most vividly about Mom during my early years was her love for her children. She thoroughly enjoyed her family and home, the preparation of nourishing soul food, meats, potatoes, vegetables and desserts for evening meals. When I came home from kindergarten at noontime I remember Mom listening regularly to her favorite radio program, "Heinie and His Grenadiers". The year was 1932, Mom was 43, and I was five years old. Mom would sing along with those German singers as well as having her own battery of songs that included some of Stephen Foster's melodies and old favorites of the era: "Silver Threads Among the Gold", "Bicycle Built for Two", and "Beautiful Dreamer", to name a few. She had a lovely voice.

My birthday, September 10, 1927, was two years before the stock market crash. My memories of growing up in Mishawaka, Indiana, are twofold as I loved so much and hated one thing! I was blessed with a wonderful loving family, my devoted and caring parents, my jovial, helpful, admirable siblings, the uniqueness and charm of a wholesome town with its many forthright people, but I hated the particular elementary school I attended.

Circa 1930 – Henry is missing

The Stock Market Crash of September 1929 was the beginning of the Great Depression that lasted for ten years. In the spring of 1932 Pop was working for a small bakery in downtown Mishawaka, The House Wife. I was just four years old at that time when the bakery went bankrupt. Pop was 49, Mom was 42, and their children ranged from 16 to 4. Months later in the fall of that year Pop found employment as the night baker for Saint Mary's College near Notre Dame at a salary of less than half of what he was earning before the depression.

The stress that Mom and Pop experienced not only included the expenses of the day, but they had consigned a friend's loan and were responsible when that friend couldn't meet his obligation. The sacrifices, the going without, that my parents had to adjust to were especially evident to my older siblings, but less so to me. I'm told that Bill's paper route money provided for some basic necessities during some of those lean times. Never sign such papers!

When I study the family portrait taken in 1923, four years before I was born, I realize what had to have been monumental adjustments for my parents and people everywhere. Most families back then had four or five children; there were seven of us to rear, feed, shelter, cloth, educate and care for. Yet, my parents managed! While Pop's two brothers, Uncle John in South Bend and Uncle Bill in Chicago, were married without children and drove new automobiles, our important machine was the Singer sewing machine. Us boys had nightgowns and under shorts made from flour sacks made by Mom at her sewing machine. In former days Mom had been accustomed to shopping at Wymans department store where fine clothing fabrics were purchased as pictured in that 1923 family portrait.

The five amiable brothers – circa 1933

My hometown, Mishawaka, in Northern Indiana, was named after an Indian princess. In the early 1930'S. the population was twenty thousand something. The main industry was a rubber plant called the Ball Band, later renamed, Uniroyal. The adjacent city, South Bend, with a population less than a hundred thousand, but growing, was home for manufacturing the Studebaker automobile. When that plant folded around 1960, South Bend ceased to grow.

Our home on Lincoln Way East was three blocks from the academically esteemed public high school, and over a mile to town center. Sections of Lincoln Way were lined with stately trees that arched together and beckoned both pedestrians and automobiles. South of town was an unspoiled hilly area referred to as, The Hills, where we youngsters went sledding after a snow fall, and it was the destination for energetic hiking on breezy balmy days. I remember Mishawaka in the 1930 as a beautiful and tranquil community with parks and the Saint Joseph River meandering through the center of this well maintained town.

Manners and decorum were established and adhered to. Chores were assigned to each of us. I learned to polish shoes along with following orders. Everyone attended to some form of school work after supper. My wardrobe was limited to several changes of garments and a necktie completed all. Clean hands and a tie were essential at the supper table.

As a youngster there were visits I made throughout the neighborhood as I was a friendly little boy. There were first, second and third generations of different nationalities, German, English, Belgian and Italians, all wonderfully warm hearted people. Our local newspaper, the South Bend Tribune, reported accidents but I don't recall reports about crime. The doors to our home were not locked day or night. Mom took charge of Pop's earnings and attended to paying all the bills. Mom kept her allocated grocery money in a soup tureen in the dining room China cabinet. Pop kept some change for streetcar fare, but Mom saw to it that he had tobacco for his pipe. There was a time when the family of one of Kate's girl friends had a struggling ice cream business and our families exchanged Pop's bread for Muldoon's heavenly ice cream!

Cheerful Jerry next to visitors auto

With four older brothers and two older sisters I learned at an early age what behavior probably wasn't going to be accepted and what was. I did have yearns for certain likings that I kept to myself. As a preschooler I was aware that my sister's dolls were for girls. There was an occurrence when I visited Kate's dolls one afternoon and probably messed them up. Kate told Mom and Mom reminded me that Kate's dolls were off limits! Thereafter all was in accord, the issue was closed. From then on I kept my guard up and I'd keep my feelings to myself! Whatever was wrong about me I'd keep to myself? I had wonderful feelings, my own private special feelings. I liked whatever it was about me and considered such feelings made me a very worthy and a loving person. Those feelings became an important part of who I am. It was with such instinctive feelings that I sometimes related to people, activities and life's environment.

By the time I was in kindergarten Pop was going to work six nights a week at Saint Mary's College, thirteen or fourteen miles from home. Around 8:30 PM

Pop boarded the street car at the end of the line which was three blocks from our home, and transferred to another streetcar in down town South Bend. He returned home every morning around seven thirty or eight. My time with him was before or after supper.

Pop was the resident barber for all, the cobbler for all, and of course all bakery goods were his specialty. Besides all that, there were the numerous ongoing and unexpected household chores that he attended to. Having playmates come to the house was fun because they took a liking to Pop and reminded me how lucky I was to have a father who enjoyed kidding about. He loved chiding the younger generation. I believe he enjoyed joshing with Kate's high school girl friends as much as anyone. When I was four and five, Pop spent time with me at my blackboard drawing human figures. I loved it and thought he was really smart!

One Christmas Eve Pop acted unusually excited and alerted everyone that he believed there might be a fire in the attic! There was much commotion to opening the attic door as it was in the upstairs hallway. Carrying the ladder through the house was part of the theatrics. All seven of us kids were crammed together in that small area as Pop got up into the attic. The moments seemed tense before he shouted, "There's no fire, but Santa Claus was here!" Then everyone started shouting "Merry Christmas!" What joy! Such a strange fuse of emotions, from fright to joy! There was the sled for one of us, and something for everyone!

When I was six, seven and eight, Pop treated me by taking me to work with him one night a year. That was a highlight to look forward to as Pop was the night baker and I'd be staying up all night! Watching Pop, the master baker working all alone in that big bakery was fun and there were lessons to be remembered. When egg shells are broken and the contents are being added to the batter, it is frequently necessary to use the index finger to clean out the entire shell. To this day my index finger is ready when cracking an uncooked egg to prevent waste. Call it ecology.

 Laundry was attended to in the basement every Monday. While we may have had a recently manufactured washer, it was nothing like today's washers and dryers. Those older machines required several large wash tubs full of water for rinsing. All that water had to be carried to an upstairs drain in the kitchen or to the yard as there were no drains in the basement. That was a regular Monday afternoon project. In nice weather the clothes were hung on the backyard clothesline, in freezing or raining weather clothes were hung in the basement.

In March 1931, Knute Rockne, the man who revolutionized the sport of football at Notre Dame was killed in a plane crash and the streets were loudly resounding to voices from mail carriers: "EXTRA EXTRA, Read All about It!! Knute Rockne killed in plane crash." In those days newspapers reached more people than radio with such startling news. This was all of twenty five years before television was a common fixture in homes, and there were many homes without radios. The Knute Rockne crash dominated the news for a long time and was thus a tragic catalyst in the progress of aviation. One significant source of change was the elimination of wood parts to metal. The progress in aviation to this 1930 era from the Wright Brother's Kitty Hawk flight in 1903 was astounding! And! In the late 1930'S., Douglas D.C. and DC3S were luxury planes connecting metropolitan areas for twenty one passengers.

Our sanctuary - home - Mishawaka, Indiana

Both parents wanted beautiful green carpet lawns, especially the front yard, and that required diligent weeding as the grade of grass seed in those days came with as much weed seed as grass seed. On occasions Mom assigned weed pulling chores for Herm, Chuck and me. We were to fill medium size buckets with weeds from the lawn before going about our free time activities. Chuck was frequently creative and filled his bucket with large weeds that he found under the shrubbery and then for appearance sake, he'd piled small weeds on top. Having done so he was happy to show off his full bucket of weeds and free to take off for the day. Whether Mom was onto Chuck and amused with his antics or simply taken in, we'll never know as Mom had a good sense of humor. Chuck always had his own unique take on all matters. When Mom was serving dessert and Pop would ask for a small piece, Chuck would exclaim, "Pop asked for a small piece and I asked for a large piece and we both have the same size!"

It was Herman who made the fervent find while digging up lawn weeds! Four years previously Mom realized that her gold wedding ring wasn't on her finger. At that time there was an ongoing search for days hoping to locate that ring. The ring had been buried in the rear garden for several years when Herman found it! No doubt he was rewarded well, perhaps with his favorite food, or excused from weed pulling so he could take off extra early for his favorite place, the Boy Scout Reservation. It was located a mile from home in a rural wooded area with a babbling creek running through the grounds. There was a cabin with living accommodations for senior scouts to maintain twenty four hour duty. The creek was dammed to create a large swimming pool with diving boards, and there were regular hours for swimming as scouts took turns at being life guards. The pool was opened in the season and during the off season the dam was dismantled. The "Scoutress," as we called it, was an important part of our early life.

The area where Herman made the "gold find" was ultimately converted to lawn for playing croquet that became an important source of recreation. There were summer afternoons when Berta made lemonade and we challenged one another on "the court". Chuck and Herm taught me how to toss and catch a ball. The neighbors welcomed seeing us in their back yard and we tossed a ball over the top of the garage from one yard to the other. When tossing we yelled, "Andy-Andy-i-over." If the throw was incomplete, we'd yell, "Pig's tail." Prior to the days of the croquet yard, the yard was a garden for growing produce. When the home garden stopped, local farmers were making regular rounds with their large or small wagons loaded with fresh vegetables and fruits. In today's world, in many communities, farmers appear on a regular weekly schedule for business, the good old fashioned way, "The Local Farmer's Markets."

A frequent occurrence that particularly stands out in my mind about the Depression Days was the number of hobos walking the streets! Until the major highway was constructed on the outskirts of town, our home was on the main thoroughfare, and the railroad was just four blocks away. Hobos appeared at our back door regularly; they were of all ages, polite and hungry. Mom usually had something to give them as one shared no matter how little one had. They probably received bread with something on it, maybe just the bread. Invariably there was a bushel of apples in the cellar so they probably got an apple. The apples were treats for after school to soothe us until supper while listening to one or two radio programs. I never imagined that we were poor because we always ate well. For me, the treat of the week was every Sunday morning as Pop made his scrumptious fresh cinnamon rolls! No one has ever baked a better roll!

As a six and seven year old I had my favorite radio programs. Tom Mix was one such program, and I listened to that on the Et Water Kent radio, one of the first radios held in high regard. It had two parts; both were metal with a gold finish. The heavy rectangular box, perhaps 8 X 12 X 18, housed many radio tubes; the separate speaker was cylinder shaped, perhaps a foot or more in height. Mom and Pop were earnest about having the "Ford Sunday Evening Hour" for all to listen to. Somehow that program with all classical music was a compensation for the phonograph player that I had been accused of breaking in a previous year. I can't recall ever being that destructive! Nevertheless, I was the fall-guy for having banished Enrico Caruso from our home. I remember how sad I was for a time having broken a ruler that cost all of one cent. Perhaps those were lessons to learn for an appreciation for the value of money. Such were the days of the Great Depression. Finding gifts for parents on special days was never complicated. For Mom it was a homemade card and a trinket that usually was for around the house. For Pop it was a homemade card with a dark chocolate Hershey bar or tobacco for his pipe.

Mr. Mumby was the pleasant man who delivered milk in the early morning several times a week regardless of weather conditions. He had a custom made milk wagon that was pulled by a faithful horse that sometimes left his calling card in the street. Saturday afternoons was collection time, Mr. Mumby was collecting for his milk delivery and Bill was collecting for his paper route. Several times a month on Saturday afternoons we heard and saw the "rag-bag-man" in his horse drawn wagon trudging down the back alley and clamoring to announce his arrival for doing business,

Pop and Henry Circa 1931

to buy your old junk for a few pennies. That alley was also the route for the ice man delivering cakes of ice for the ice-box.

This was an era that seemed to me to have minimum change around town. For years the U. S. Post Office delivered mail twice a day and all for a three cent stamp! When the government changed that tender to four cents, it appeared that the country was in a crisis. Henry wrote in his autobiography that the Ivy League Schools in the Northeast were scouting for likely candidates to receive scholarships. Money was so tight at that time that he didn't apply because there were no visible funds for transportation even though tuition would be paid. He settled for a university a hundred plus miles from home.

As a youngster I was a born naturalist. I loved exploring creatures of nature, creatures in the air or crawling insects or digging up worms. I caught butterflies, bumblebees, grasshoppers and fire flies. I'd catch them in bottles and let them go after I had studied them. I dug up earthworms for the neighbors next

25

Circa 1937: Fives sets of different genes!

door who went fishing. They were a childless couple and they treated me as if I belonged to them. Fortunately I never got too attached to stray dogs or cats as they never stayed around for any time.

During that kindergarten year I yearned to have my own beautiful goldfish. When Mom and I were shopping at the local dime store, Mom bought for me the most beautiful goldfish I'd ever seen! That was so special! This was the age when I constructed a "May Altar" with a figurine of the Blessed Virgin that I purchased with my own money that I earned by attending to chores for the neighbors. The shrine was placed in the dining room and I adorned it for the entire month with flowers from the garden and wild flowers from nearby fields. It was my own special doing and it was revered and beautiful. Another special day during those early years was when the neighbors who fished with my worms gave me a beautiful bright yellow canary in a choice cage with all the trimmings! I treasured that bird because it was so beautiful to look at and it was a part of nature that I had grown to love. Throughout childhood I had a passion to know life. No one loved exploring more than I and hiking and bicycling became my passion at an early age.

There were no formal, no specific lessons, regarding human reproduction. There was the realization, a given, that there are two sexes with different anatomies. The facts of biology were referenced at appropriate times from those informed, usually family. My curiosity was acknowledged and there wasn't any sexual abuse nor playing around among us siblings. I remember preparing for bed as a time with frequent joshing with silly dares. "Go to the head of the stairs and yell down to Mom: "Mom! Mom! I can't find my! — Oh, Oh, here it is!" With reference to finding my nightgown. At times we boys were amused with such triviality as we were always looking for something to laugh about. I believe Mom was pleased that we enjoyed our laughs.

When Chuck was in Cub Scouts he took on a project of making a scrap book about Chicago gangsters. Dillinger was the big focus of the time and the newspapers were full of stories and photographs of his every action. I was happy to be constructive and felt important to be helping this big brother find pictures in the newspaper and then cut them out for this very important project! As a little kid and also as an adult, projects have always energized me. At age six or seven I got carried away with the idea of planting my own treasure chest. Chuck helped me. Off in a corner of the backyard we dug a hole some fifteen or twenty inches deep in which I carefully placed "The Chest," a tin can of sorts, with choice castoff "treasures." I can't recall what those valuable treasures were, but the thought that someday someone would discover them had great appeal to my imagination. I must confess that there were occasions when I was compelled to unearth the treasure to make sure that it was still intact. Mom rewarded my adventuresome spirit by assigning a small parcel of garden whereby I planted my own seeds and cultivated them.

Chuck was always good at helping his kid brother. For a time we arranged a theater in a basement room where we presented "Shadow Shows," always an after dark production. On one side of the white sheet curtain we arranged seating for our audience. We loved it when we had a packed house of more than seven. Stage lights had to be appropriately placed to cast a shadow onto the curtain, so we were our own electrical engineers. One of our skits was titled: "The Operation." We took turns playing the doctor and the patient in this hospital setting. The patient was lying on the operating table with the silhouette of his body reflecting on the curtain while the doctor wheeled a very large knife performing the operation. After the elaborate incision the doctor reached into the patient's stomach and pulled out all sorts of debris, taking his time to do so; there was an assortment of tools intertwined with long ropes all conveniently stashed in a drawer of the operating table. The skit was concluded when the doctor thrusts his hand through the curtain holding a can and proudly announces: "It's a can, Sir!"

In second grade I walked home from school with two brothers. They lived a few blocks beyond my house and we played at each other's homes. Our luncheons at school were always bagged from home and we frequently exchanged sandwiches. They liked my peanut butter and jelly sandwiches on Pop's bread, and I thought their store bought bread with mayonnaise was something unusual; certainly it was different for me. I liked visiting their home and seeing the extraordinary craftsmanship their dad did to make their home beautiful. It was a sad day, a day of humiliation, for us children when they were forced to move out of that home because there were bills they couldn't pay. Sometime later I bicycled to their new location in South Bend and there I heard Mr. Smith mournfully bad mouthing the Mishawaka officials who were responsible for his losing his beautiful home. The Smiths were typical of many families throughout the country who lost their home during the depression years.

I don't believe my parents had any serious arguments or show of temper, but with one exception. Pop had an aversion to curry and once when Mom inadvertently used more of that spice than she might have, Pop made it known that curry didn't belong in our kitchen! Aside from that, Pop was always helping in one way or another. I can clearly envision him at the kitchen sink washing dishes while Kate and Berta were drying. Pop would say that Mom worked very hard preparing supper and we should all help afterwards. When Kate and Berta dried dishes they frequently sang songs. One song that I can't forget was sung with a slow sweet melodious rhythm —

> "The east bound train was crowded, one cold December day.
> The conductor shouted tickets, in his good old fashion way.
> There was a little girl, who said, "I have no ticket",
> And thus her story told. My father..."

I don't recall the on-going words, but I remember making up my own renditions and they weren't always pretty, but I believed them to be poetic and I felt the pains of laughter in my groin. My lyrics usually had all kinds of wild conventionalities for mother, father, brother sister, from being lost or going down below, or going up above to heaven or being some sort of derelict, vagabond. My versions usually ended with: "And where I'll go nobody knows!"

Pop always knew how to express himself without vulgar language, but there were a few cuss words when his sanity was impinged upon during the task of wallpapering our three bed room home. When the job was finished he did realize the satisfaction of a job well done. His work was perfection. Our house had central heating from a coal burning furnace in the basement. One year after a very frigid winter it was necessary to redo the wallpaper above the floor furnace vent where the paper was abused. That "warming station" was a reckoning spot for us youngsters to warm our fanny; while standing there our fannies played war on the wallpaper. That didn't happen another winter season.

When I was eight the entire décor of our downstairs was completely changed. The large framed photographs of our grandparents measuring 20 X 30 were relegated to the attic and replaced with colorful landscape prints. Paternal grandparents had hung in the living room, maternal grandparents hung in the dining room. I liked the new cheerful décor. I was with Mom when she purchased the new wallpaper, and in a way, I felt somewhat responsible having made the big change that beautified our home.

Our home was always clean, but it was immaculately clean for Sundays as Mom and Pop followed the Dutch tradition for cleanliness. General house cleaning was attended to every Saturday morning. It was Bill who would throw out the question, "What war did General House Cleaning fight in?" Herman, Chuck and I took the area rugs to the backyard clothesline to beat them with a wire beater. Yep! My parents followed the Dutch tradition of cleanliness.

The unusual joyous and sad days are the ones that particularly stand out in one's memories. It was truly a sad day when Mom had a wretched accident by spilling a kettle of boiling water on her legs. Mom had to sit in a chair for days until the large blisters healed! Berta became the breakfast chef, hot oatmeal, milk or cocoa, toast and jam. Either Pop or Berta prepared supper as both enjoyed having their culinary skills critiqued. With such a large brood as we were, Kate also did her share. However, having had polio as a two year old and an ongoing challenge with corrective shoes, she was rather fragile. Berta was always there for Kate as she had a zeal and fervor for challenges. During her entire life Berta enjoyed cooking and sewing as much as she enjoyed reading.

There was a schedule for each day of the week and for each hour of the day. Supper was served regularly at six o'clock and grace was said before and after eating. There was no eating and running. With dessert came a degree of relaxation and the customary animated conversation. After each of us had a voice the table was cleared for school homework. When the dishes were washed and put away, some in the kitchen cabinet, others in the built in dining room China cabinet, Mom and Pop reclined in their respective living room chairs. The afternoon newspaper was there and the library books that Berta brought home were attended to. Pop liked reading European history and Mom liked travel books. Berta enjoyed reading aloud and I liked her loving attention. .

Mom – circa 1938

Perhaps these were among the happiest days of Mom's life; married for 27 years, widowed for 25 years and died at age 77. There was the obvious stress regarding the slim income that required lowering standards for many expectations, she never the less achieved a worthy station with a loving husband and the rearing of seven healthy, happy children. When Henry came home from DePauw University on occasional weekends (with his dirty laundry), it was a joyous time for everyone, especially for Mom! It was 1935, the middle of the Great Depression.

My Accounting of Grade School and Church

*Somehow we learn who we really
are then live with that decision.*
Eleanor Roosevelt

Saint Joseph School was adjacent to the parish church, the priest rectory, the nuns convent, and directly across Fourth Street was Saint Joseph Hospital in downtown Mishawaka, Indiana. The school grounds were not extensive to provide a play yard, so the side street next to the school was blocked during recess hours with wooden horses. There were two other Catholic parishes in Mishawaka, several public grade schools and one public high school. Geographically, the city limits met those of South Bend and the University of Notre Dame was near.

I attended kindergarten at the public school just one block from home and enjoyed those morning sessions. There was one occasion when I was sent to the cloak room for some misbehaving.

From my siblings I learned about Saint Joseph School, one and a half mile from home, and was excited to be following in their footsteps. However, that reality

was short lived. I did not like first grade. My feelings went from downhearted to spiritless. Sometimes I thought the teacher treated us like babies, other times I thought she was mean. I knew I didn't like her for whichever reasons. Pop and Mom thought I'd be alright with a different teacher in second grade.

Whatever the cause, I did not assimilate the lessons as put forth by those nuns. Most of them were younger and perhaps had less training than the ones that taught my older siblings, or they came from devastating backgrounds. In those days, the 1920'S. and 30'S, as Henry states, there were as many as forty to fifty pupils per class with one nun/teacher. In my opinion the nuns that were assigned me had little training to be teaching children in any classroom.

In his autobiography Henry wrote about his experiences at Saint Joseph School and said that all six of his siblings followed the same path that he experienced. He wrote: "They were happy years for all of us!" That statement is certainly not true for any of us! A greater degree of dissatisfaction followed all six of us siblings, to where I was constantly questioning and defying those nun/teachers in the privacy of my mind. I frequently had an upset stomach and Mom would have Dr. Wygant stop on his way home. I was good business for the Pepto-Bismol industry. As for curing those classroom stomach and head aches, naps at home were customary as home was a sanctuary where hours fleeted while hours in the classroom seemed endless.

My undiagnosed disability caused painful learning blocks. Pop sat with me nightly for five years going through the assigned reading lessons. I spent two full years in second grade and two full years in third grade, detesting all ten years at Saint Joe. Without a doubt it was Pop who was responsible for my having acquired a sight vocabulary as focusing and retention were difficult. Thanks to Pop's patience I acquired border-line reading skills that allowed me to squeeze by. After supper, evening after evening, at the dining room table for fifteen or twenty minutes, I was scrutinizing the letters in the words and trying to remember three and four letter words. Although I felt demoralized within the confines of the school for having been held back, I refused to allow that to dictate my worth. I felt that I had a premonition about life, a grip, deeper ideas than others had, even those nuns! In my heart I knew I wasn't unintelligent.

There were many instances of humiliation that compounded my disability. When I didn't respond as expected, the nun would then instruct the class: "Look at Gerald." I would be standing as we always stood when called upon, when she'd say: "Gerald didn't study his catechism last night! Gerald's brother always did his homework and he's in college! Now, once more, Gerald, what are the ten commandments?" Or, "Who made you," and the answer had to be worded as in the catechism. Such comparisons with siblings were frequent and usually made during catechism class, the first lesson of the day. Some of those un qualified, delusional, nuns believed that shaming was motivating.

For ten long years I heard about the wonderful man called the Pope. He was infallible in telling everyone what God wants everyone to do to save his immortal soul, because he had a direct line to God that went all the way back to Saint Peter. This Pope didn't have to go through God the son, Jesus, he went directly to God the Father. Then there was the ghost god. God the Holy Ghost, he had one particular job, to ascend upon you during Confirmation and provide you with good energy to live a good Catholic life. Somehow, all three gods, the father, son, and the ghost all shared the same package, the same spirit called The Trinity. This was the one true god that created the world and had a snake tell Adam's wife, Eve, the first woman, not to eat a particular apple. Eve committed a sin by disobeying and ate the apple. If Eve had obeyed the snake the world wouldn't know suffering and it would be a much happier place. It was the likes of such "teaching" that prompted unconfined hours of philosophical quandary during those formative years.

The concept of "eternity" as taught, gave rise to much thought. Since a person's body and soul are connected as one entity, and that entity began when being born into this world, why would it be judged, damned to hell or saved in heaven, for an "eternity" because it did or didn't follow "their rules?" I knew, intrinsically, that I had soul, spirit, but rejected what those nuns expounded on.

Once on the trek home from school my chums and I went into a Lutheran Church where religious films were being shown; such a treat for us! When the nuns heard about our debauchery we were lectured as though we had committed a grievous crime, a real sin against the Pope and God! In those days a mortal sin could send you to hell for eternity! And! That is the reason why it is so important not to miss mass on Sundays or on Holy Days of Obligation, or eat meat on Fridays! That would be a mortal sin and if you died with a mortal sin on your soul, you'd spend eternity in hell! Eternity, yet! As Catholics we did have obligations!

The tentacles of control were far reaching. The procession of crazed authorization came from the Vatican, the diocese, the local parish. Under the pains of hell the church banded the reading of particular books or seeing certain films; at death, cremation was prohibited. There was a restriction on Catholics who wanted to be in a wedding party if that ceremony was held in a Protestant Church. Father Lauer, our senior pastor, had a rule that parents must send their children to the parish school if they wanted to receive Holy Communion. Of course that restriction was lifted when the obstreperous kids got expelled from Saint Joe.

Such were some of the playing rules under the guise of guidance; there were many more "must do, must believe," to save your soul. How I pined for those church services with the priest's uninspiring dry readings of the gospels to be over! Additionally, what I thought to be hocus-pocus were taught as articles of faith revealed by God and were required believing.

Baptism is a church Sacrament to cleanse the soul form original sin. (?) The church teaches that it is necessary to be Baptized to enter heaven. Different popes declared that the Virgin Mary, mother of the son of God, Jesus, was born without this original sin. The Vatican believed they unveiled an "infallible truth" and made mandatory beliefs to celebrates her Feast Days, The Immaculate Conception and The Assumption of Mary are holy days of obligation.

Before school every day we attended mass and on Sundays we were to attend children's mass. I hated going to children's mass where adults were also present. I was a head taller than my classmates and that compounded my hate for Saint Joe. On Monday mornings the nun wanted to know why someone was not with the class. I would lie and say that I went to the adult's high mass when actually I was out enjoying God's nature on my bicycle. I had identified with some Protestants friends who didn't have such rules of sin and more sin! There were times when I went to the adult mass where adults paid ten cents for pew rental, a common practice in many churches during the Great Depression. To show leadership, our pastor, Father Lauer, compiled a yearly publication showing the tithing that each family made. His book keeping was distributed to the congregation. (I always had something of a serious nature to think about.)

"Holy Communion" was just that! It was not symbolic of receiving the body and blood of Jesus Christ; it was and still is considered receiving the REAL flesh and blood of Jesus! All this changing was (and is) a miracle that was granted to the priest when he was ordained a priest. Two of his fingers are consecrated that allowed him to change the bread, a wafer, into the host which becomes the flesh of Jesus. If by accident the host fell only a priest could pick it up. That wafer on your tongue or on the floor was the real body of Jesus Christ! Many Catholic Churches did away with serving wine, or blood, and only served the host, the body, --the flesh of Jesus!

At Saint Joseph's Church the third graders learned to make their first Holy Communion. The previous year, the second graders were taught how to go to Confession. We were taught to enter the confessional, kneel and say: "Bless me father for I have sinned. My last confession was (name the time) and I've committed the following sins. The nun in charge of teaching would have all second grade pupils put their heads down, nestled in their folded arms with eyes closed, while she read each of the Ten Commandments and their implied ramifications, and explained the intended meaning. The entire process might have taken from fifteen to thirty minutes. The first Commandments that dealt with the love for God and keeping the Sabbath Holy, opened up the nuns take on God, The Church and the Pope. We were warned of the importance to never, never, make a bad comment about the Church, or its priests or nuns. If one said anything unkind or untrue they would receive severe punishment from God at some point in their life. I don't recall any lessons from the priest in the confessional, but I remember the usual absolutions. For penance say three Hail Marys and four Our Fathers. The advise was: " Try to not think about such things."

Addressing the seventh commandment, "Thou shall not commit adultery," introduced the subject of one's genitals. Here again the nun read from the instructional Confessional booklet "Did I touch myself in an impure place?" And then she'd try to explain and say, you know what I mean. Just what was sin and what was acknowledging one's body "in an impure place"?

First Communion - Fasted from midnight

There was teaching of how to have a happy death. The rationale was that one wouldn't be in any prolonged suffering when the soul reached the other side; it (or you/me) wouldn't have to spend a lot of time in purgatory. To assure, hopefully, the granting of such blessings it was important to have received Holy Communion on a series of Good Fridays, the first Friday of each month, for one year. To establish good religious habits, all the children in the school went to confession on Thursday before Good Friday and communion on Good Friday. I rejected what I was expected to be learning about the church as far back as first grade. If we were created in the image of God, why were we born with original sin on our soul? Our religious lessons were habitually coupled with the wages of sin, mortal, the big one and venial, the lesser one. We were frequently instructed about mysteries of the church and the importance to believe in them.

The nuns that reigned and proselytized at this time, the ones that I had, were so embroiled with the idea that the Catholic Church was the one and only true religion. The Protestants churches were founded by men; the Catholic Church was founded by Jesus Christ, God's son, (as taught in the Apostles' Creed) and Saint Peter. Those nuns were most adamant with their concern that the church was constant in its spiritual teaching from the day of its conception, two thousand years ago, and would remain constant until the end of time.

It would be interesting if those same nuns could explain why the church has been granting marriage annulments for the last forty years. Those abiding by the church's rules in previous generations had to remain single if they wanted to go to heaven! Just recently, in the beginning of this 21st century, the church allowed for the discontinuing of that place called "purgatory," such an avowed segment of the catechism in my youth! Purgatory was a "holding station" to do penance before entering heaven. And today, even lay-people without those consecrated fingers are allowed to handle the host–the real flesh of Jesus!

It was tradition for Saint Joe to have an afternoon costume carnival in the school's auditorium at Halloween time. During my second year in third grade I dressed up like a teenage girl. I had all the paraphernalia: a flower print dress, pretty shoes, a large wig with a sun bonnet type hat and lipstick. I suspected that my teacher nun wouldn't approve so I avoided the classroom and went directly to the carnival hall. I believed myself to be mysterious as I embellished my ideas of a flirtatiously coy girl, with girly body gestures. I had fun imagining that this could be another me! I was rather satisfied that the nuns didn't approve. I believe psychologists would refer to such actions as acting out an alter ego, the feminine side of my male psyche. There were no further attempts at any time in my life to be in drag. I always wanted to present myself as a regular guy.

I believe that this particular episode was a turning point for me in getting to understand myself more thoroughly. My perception for knowing who I am was beginning to come full circle. The excitement, the fathoming of getting a handle at self understanding took a form of enchanted discernment that I absorbed intuitively. This responsive aspect of my makeup, my Gay gene, was never overstated and I believe I presented myself having a masculine demeanor to ward off suspicions of a Gay gene. Especially important in those days!

My hatred for Saint Joe grew deeper with this second year in third grade. I should have been with classmates in the fifth grade and I was grouped with younger children who could read better than I. Even if Mom and Pop sent me to the public school, at this late date, I would be embarrassed having the kids I went to kindergarten see me so far behind. Playground time was just as degrading as being in class. I didn't join the boy classmates playing games using sticks instead of balls. They were younger and they played rough. I passed the recess time by interacting with a bunch of girls. There was always silly stuff to talk about. My behavior was not to the nun's liking. On occasions she made assignments for the entire class that would keep them busy so she would be free to discipline me in the hall outside the classroom door. That was her private counseling station for many of us pupils. It was there that she ordered me, but to no avail, to stop visiting with the girls on the playground. Furthermore, I was not to walk home from school with so and so and I should be with so and so. I was repeatedly assured that she and the other nuns didn't approve of me.

The mores of the day were a favorite topic for those nuns to vent upon before their young charges. When I was in my first year of third grade the nun got off onto the subject of people's first names. She found it virtually sinful that some parents would name their children after a movie star, like Shirley Temple, instead of a saint's name. I still remember seeing classmate Shirley Breiler's eyes swell up with tears as the nun ranted on. And, there was the eighth or seventh grade nun who got off onto seething rampages of pregnant brides at the altar! The demoralizing mores of the day actually extended right there to their convent mother house! What is happening to society when young novitiates joining their religious order needed a smoking room where they could go to break their dirty habit?

My parents left the training of Catholicism to the school. At home there was the subscription to the Sunday Visitor, a Catholic paper, but no Bible. There was the customary before and after meal prayer. I don't recall any stimulating references to the Church or the Bible. Showing concern for others was the religion that my parents professed. About the time I was born Pop and Mom were caring for Uncle Carl who had a losing fight with the demons of alcohol. Carl's wife, mother of two, purchased travel fare from Holland to send Carl to Pop, his brother. It was believed that Pop, if anyone, could help. After a brief time, both Pop and Uncle Carl lost their plight.

In our adult years, Herman told me that there were frequent times when the nuns put him and Ralph Ganser down. As it developed he and Ralph were the only ones in their large class who went on to earn college degrees. Herm, like Chuck, was not one to criticize, but when he got started on Saint Joe it was a litany of woes. In my opinion, for every honor roll student in high school that was enrolled at St. Joe, there were more than an average number of screwed up individuals that had gone to St. Joe. Thus, I take umbrage with Henry's exalted opinion of that school back in those days.

I don't recall Chuck complaining about the nuns even though he wasn't enjoying schoolwork. It seems that he and a few buddies just ignored the nuns and went quietly their own way. Chuck was his own proud person and wouldn't let the nuns or anyone dictate his self-worth. It wasn't important if he spoke proper grammar, so much the better if it was funny and if it felt good, he'd relished it. While the nuns lost Chuck, T. V. Comedy Central had a forerunner in Chuck.

Weeks before her death, and what would have been her ninetieth birthday, Kate and I reminisced via phone. She enjoyed remembering the love in our family and the caring she gave to me when I was young. When Kate was just two years old she contacted polio that affected one of her legs and her ability to walk normally. She recalled how both parents were so attentive to bathing that leg. When she was in the fifth grade she had a foot operation that required wearing a custom made shoe. Kate talked about her unforgettable experience that took place when that shoe came off accidentally.

She and classmates were climbing the steps to the church's choir loft when the boy behind her stepped on the heel of that shoe and it slipped off. Several boys picked it up and amused themselves by passing it all around when the nun realized that there was some irregularity. The boy's fun was abruptly stopped when the nun retrieved the shoe and returned it to Kate along with a hard slap across the face! Kate had regrets that she didn't tell Pop. In retrospect she realizes that Pop would have paid the nun a visit despite his usual assumption that the nuns were always fair and honest. Such faith in the nuns was so true of most parents. In her adulthood and during the last days of life, Kate could not forget the feel of that slap!

As an adult I conjure up the circuitry of those nuns as follows: Henry fell into that percentage that was easily pliable academically and the likes of him were cowed into being a goody-goody and therefore favored. (I remember how the nuns favored that minority.) Kate's group was not quite as pliable and too large to receive individual acknowledgment; they were treated with reserved tolerance. I fell into a group that was chastised for not conforming academically nor behaviorally. Today, three quarters of a century later, such discipline would be considered child abuse. As unbelievable as it may seem, those nuns were provided an environment that enabled them to vent their frustrations.

My sentiments as opposed to Henry's allegiance to Saint Joe, are those of overcrowded classrooms that were like barricades in a secure militaristic compound, where the majority of nun/teachers were drill sergeants setting an example to the vulnerable young to become control freaks as servants for God. These nuns took vows to be brides of Jesus. The Apostles' Creed teaches that Jesus is God's son. I do believe that some of those nuns theorized that their father-in-law was God! Today, there are no nun teachers at Saint Joe. The mother house for that order of nuns has been converted to a two year liberal college.

During the 30s and early 40s I was aware of the disparaging attitude that my nun teachers held toward the Protestant Churches. To a much lesser degree there was an attitude of condescension between many Christian Churches in those days. Each denomination had its bias for being different from the others. As my nun teachers looked down on other Christian denominations, the Baptist, Episcopal, Lutheran, Methodist, Presbyterian and others, I looked all about and I knew that this Catholic Church wasn't for me! I can still hear those shrill voices emphatically exclaiming the horrors of God's beloved angel, Lucifer. It was Lucifer who turned on God, declared war, and became hell's ruling devil who wants everyone's soul! (It takes faith to believe in the devil.)

For some Christians the Apostle's Creed remains an essential part of their beliefs. It is an adaptation of the Nicene Creed which was composed 325 A.D. and was recited from memory. It is the story of the ghost God impregnating a young girl, Mary, who became the birth mother to Jesus; Jesus being the son in the Trinity, the Father, Son and the Holy Ghost. It was God the father who created everything, heaven, earth, hell. This father God loved us humans so much that he sent Jesus to be crucified to atone for yours and my sins! Jesus will return on judgment day and our bodies will be resurrected so we can have lasting life either in heaven or the fires in hell! Such is an idolater's mosaic! It was repugnant to me as a youngster and appalling to me as a spiritual seeker!

This creed and other teachings became a morbid part of my day at Saint Joe, leaving me feeling, at times, dreary and jaundiced. It was important to remember if you ever have to decide between denying the Catholic Church's teachings, or death, chose death because you'll go straight to heaven! In the 1930s and early 40s many Christian Churches taught that you had to be baptized to be "saved." As a first grader I felt the cruelty of such a dehumanizing thought because I had imagined many people were not baptized. At Saint Joseph, we were taught that God favored us because we were born Catholic! We were reminded to believe, to have faith. Faith is belief because you're brainwashed to believe.

It is tradition for the congregations in many Christian Churches to recite this Apostle's Creed in unison. I can only imagine that it is recited mindlessly as a form of tradition. For me it has always professed absurdities: The Holy Trinity, the incarnation, the nativity, the passion of Christ, the resurrection, the atonement, and the judgement of the living and the dead! Our social mores are so structured that it is expedient to join the chorus than to question such supernaturalism. I believe that this Creed exemplifies sacred tyranny. It is an aside from Jesus' insightful teachings as a "way shower!" He was a humanitarian, a humanist. This creed compounded my aversion for St Joseph's school.

As a very young child I had an affinity to love life and its creator. I entertained numerous possibilities what God was and what life was all about. One of my favorite crystallizations was that I was an "old soul" having been born many times, like plant seeds, divine inherent, and that this life was an assignment that was handed to me, or one that I chose. Saint Joe was my assignment, my challenge! I had theories galore for the meaning of life! Coming into existence and possibly spending eternity in a miserable place called hell because you didn't live by their rules, their Catechism, had to be crazy thinking, and people who believed that were misguided, dumb, and stupid! I believe that my equilibrium was kept in check with the likes of such inferences and my own spiritual beliefs.

Ever since I could remember I knew that someday I'd have a male partner and that too didn't fit into their beliefs. In my dreams I caressed a boyfriend and I couldn't accept the idea that was a sin. In my heart I knew what these "religious people" were expounding on couldn't possibly be my Creator's love for me! After ten long dreary years at Saint Joseph School, my eighth grade diploma had the words, "Satisfactorily Completed," crossed out! Nevertheless, that day was one of the happiest days of my life!

Grade VI Feb 19, 1941

The world is — kind of a spiritual kindergarten where millions of bewildered infants are trying to spell God with the wrong blocks.

Edwin A. Robinson

The best that some of us can expect on the Day of Judgment is a suspended sentence.

When you get to heaven you will be surprised to see many people there you did not expect to see. Many will be just as surprised to see you there!

Man can live without air for a few minutes, without food for six weeks, and without a new thought for a lifetime.

Ice skating in the park - Mishawaka

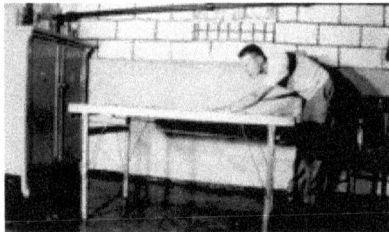

Aiming the ball in basement recreation room

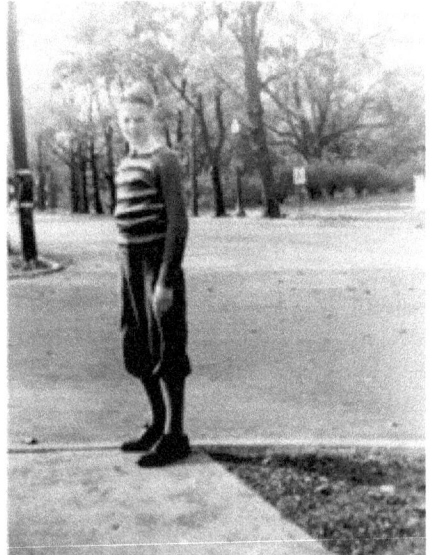

Me in school dress, knickers of era, circa, 1938

The five brothers - "M" for Mishawaka High

Boy Scout Reservation-all dammed up

Puberty

Puberty is a stage of life defined in biological terms. Adolescence is the period from the beginning of puberty to the attainment of maturity. For many people their sexual orientation is shaped during these dynamic years of puberty. Psychologists agree that for the most part sexual identity comes through a complex interaction of (1) biological (2) psychological and (3) social factors. Science hasn't identified any one single component causing homosexuality. My belief favors "biological inheritance" as the dominant factor regarding my Gay gene. I believe the genetic components, the developmental stage of the sperm and the uniqueness of the egg are the main determinates for my homosexual orientation. No doubt my negative experiences in grade school helped expedite my inevitable sexual development.

It was 1940, 41, when I was 12 and 13 years old, in the 5th and 6th grades when I began puberty. My intense feelings of dislike for those nuns grew proportionally. I was a head taller with hairy legs and a face with acne as defined from my younger classmates. Worst than being the tallest in the classroom and always lining up at the end of the line as was the custom was the idea, supposedly, that being held back denoted lack of intelligence. I never accepted any such idea for myself, but I supposed some people thought that of me. I usually related well with class leaders and having their goodwill kept me from acting out as I was tempted to do more often than not. Nevertheless it was embarrassing to be grouped with younger classmates who were good readers while I stumbled with reading. When learning was to please the teacher/nun, I had no particular desire to please. Exerting a small degree of independence seemed important.

I had strong crushes on boys my age as far back as I can remember. As a six and seven year old I had playmates of both sexes, but my desire to hug special boyfriends was powerful. I never desired to hug a girl friend at any age. During these early years, when I was 4, 5 and 6 years old, I remember getting into bed and deciding between two choices to put me to sleep. Either hugging my pillow and pretending that it was my special boy friend, or programming my dream to take me on a particular adventure. Such dreaming was natural because it was like seeing a motion picture at a movie theater. As a preschooler I became aware that I was more sensitive, more instinctive, sympathetic and caring than other boys. I knew I was different! I was different and I liked who I was in spite of everything at Saint Joseph's School.

Beginning in first grade I experienced learning blocks. Among my varied quandaries, especially in later years, has been my wondering if there was some disconnection in the brain. I felt the hurt pride in not meeting expectations regarding focusing. The pressure on me to be otherwise was met with growing dislike for those nuns. In my quandary I ask some of the following questions. Was my desire for hugging a boyfriend, having a gay gene, and receptive learning, not in accord with sexual orientation in the brain? Perhaps a "learning block" was connected to being different? Could it be that the dye was set for a "gay gene" at the time of conception? Could it be the nun's proselytizing that I could not endure that prompted lack of concentration, an attention deficit? Some religious stories at this very early age were upsetting and caused pain. Could it be that I had conflicting beliefs carried over from a former life? Insanity? Crazy? Leave all such speculation to medical researchers, the sociologists. In due time, years from now, their findings, including birth order, will be more thoroughly studied. Focusing to learn, to learn reading, still has unfinished research.

With various stages of puberty the mind as well as the body changes. The thinking seeks a degree of independence. At no time did I accept that I had a deficient mind. In the middle grades I believed I had a discerning mind and occasionally imagined that I was celestially inspired. I questioned my limitations but never accepted defeat. I appreciated the talents I possessed and believed I could perceive matters of spirituality contrary to those being taught.

My serious interests in psychology developed during early puberty, age 12, 13, 14, while in 5th, 6th, and 7th grades as I was strongly attracted to boys. Simultaneously, I felt connected spiritually to God, but adamantly rejected what I was hearing in the classroom regarding church teaching and sin. I frequently imagined I had a calling to a ministerial life. I contacted a religious brother at the University of Notre Dame and we had an hour's visit. I gained some ideas of what I might expect in such a religious order, and left after a warm embrace and a kiss on the forehead. My interests in a ministerial life continued for some years as I learned about Buddhism and conjectured what life as a Buddhist monk would be like. The Beatitudes that are credited to Jesus, are in part, taken from The Eight-fold Path of Buddhism, the profoundly human understanding of virtue at its best!

At this stage I entertained a wide range of ideas. My intuitiveness was my vanguard. I wondered if men who felt spiritual were in a category whereby it was natural for them to be drawn to men of like mind. More than yearning to associate with a religious creed, I desired a life surrounded by loving male companionship. Perhaps a spiritual path could offer that. I was gaining a better understanding of myself with a source of authorization to be myself. I liked and respected myself even more as I always knew I would.

We are Spiritual Beings Having a Human Experience

Life is like a game of cards. The hand that is dealt is determinism; the way you play it is free will.   Jawaharlal Nehru

Men have fiendishly conceived a heaven only to find it insipid, and a hell to find it ridiculous.   George Santayana

Any fool can make a rule, and any fool can mind it.   Henry D. Thoreau

All you need is ignorance and confidence and the success is sure.
Mark Twain

When I do good, I feel good; when I do bad, I feel bad, and that is my religion.
Abraham Lincoln

Your daily life is your temple and religion. -------

When we die we leave behind all that we have and take with us all that we are.
Kahlil Gibran

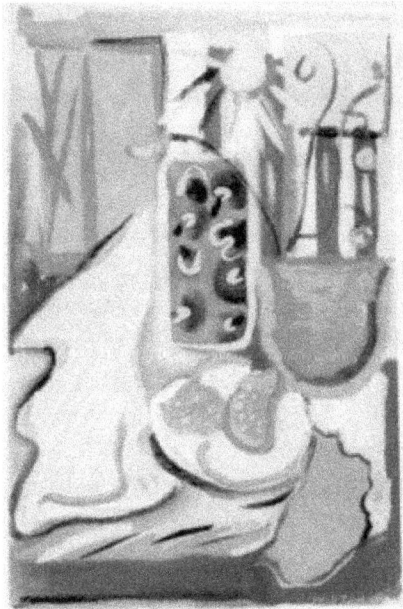

My Abstract -
Acrylic, circa 1955

If you're going through hell, keep going.
Winston Churchill

Don't aim to be an earthly Saint with eyes fixed on a star. Just try to be the fellow that you Mother thinks you are.   Will S. Adkin

Here lies my Past, Good-bye I have kissed it, Thank you, kids, I wouldn't have missed it.   Ogdon Nash

Pop's Death and My Siblings

Pearl Harbor, December 7, 1941, and the following years brought about frequent changes to our home. On that momentous day Pop had just heard the news on radio when I walked into the house. We were alone. Pop was expressionless for a time and then shared the horrible news! Later when Mom arrived and learned the disastrous revelations, there was a veil of silence followed with depression and concern! It had not been many years since the horrors of World War One were known to them. Now, Mom and Pop had children who would be of military age. Henry was already in the Naval Midshipmen School, and Bill had joined the army after his graduation from high school. Soon thereafter a scroll with two stars hung in the living room bay window. All families throughout the country with sons and daughters in the military hung such a scroll to show pride and patriotism. Months later there were four stars on that scroll!

One year after Pearl Harbor, in November '42, Pop died of cancer. Had he sought medical treatment sooner than he did, he would have had a longer life span. Pop was just sixty years old and Mom was a widow at age fifty three. I was just fourteen. Some of the first words that Mom said to me after she was told of Pop's death were, "I'm happy that you got to know your father." In those days a wake was held in the home before the coffin was taken to the church for a funeral mass. Those days were of homage and reflection.

I suppose there are some who would chide me, the youngest of seven, as being spoiled. I did receive much attention, but then, we all were mindful of one another as were our parent's core value of "Caring!" A few times Chuck, Herm and I pondered the idea if our parents had favorites; if so, was Henry favored? If he was, that was okay because, after all, he was their first.

Pop, taking a breather with pipe & book circa 1941

44

Henry (12-25-15): With a twelve year age difference my recollections of Henry before he left home for college are few. I may have been age four when I was curious about the game that encompassed Henry's and Pop's attention. They were playing chess and I watched for a time. All types of board and card games were housed in the bottom section of the built in China cabinet in the dining room and Henry knew them all. In college he was elected to the Phi Beta Kappa national honor society. When I was twelve and Henry was living in a rooming house in Chicago while teaching at De Paul University, he had me visit him for four or five days. The one hundred mile bus trip and our time together, visiting the zoo, the Museum of Science and Industry, the Art Museum, was a big adventure! When I was sixteen and he was a Midshipman in the Navy, I was his best man at his church wedding in August 1943, to Victoria Szaulewicz Shelley. Vicky was born and raised in South Bend. Their marriage produced one daughter, Emily, son, Edward, and identical twins, Victor and Hank. Henry's life work was in the field of actuarial science. He retired as president of an insurance company. His transition was in 2004

Alberta (2-21-17): Berta was ten and a half years older and believed me to be a very bright person. Her birth placement set her up as Mom's right hand helper, so she, like Mom, had an early influence on me. Berta was a zealous reader who affiliated with classical literature. She loved reading to me and telling me about the world figures she admired. I don't recall any expounding on religion, per se, but she loved talking about her hero, Albert Schweitzer (1875-1965). I believe she read all of his books about his medical life in Africa. He was a profound figure in his day as a humanitarian, scientist, and philosopher. The hikes that Berta and I took are a memorable part of my early years. A one way hike from our home to Notre Dame was over ten miles. We'd do that and then comb the campus before returning home. Berta earned her R.N. degree from the local nursing school and then located to Chicago where she had an eventful life at hospital nursing and being an American Air Line "hostess," as they were called when flying the DC 3'S. May 43, she married Dr. William Hambley. He was doing his medical residency and they were married in the courthouse. For them to have been married by a Catholic priest meant that Bill would have had to sign papers promising to raise their children Catholic. Bill refused. Bill was raised in Pikeville, Kentucky. They had four children, two daughters two sons, Mary, JR., Barbara and John. Her transition was in 1976.

Catherine (9-21-18): The influence of two older sisters who were so different, yet so close, must have registered with me. Both had a love for semantics that played out during their lifetime visits where they challenged one another with scrabble. Kate enjoyed contemporary novels and current events. Berta identified with classical literature and history. Kate would pride herself at being competitive and playing bridge was her favorite forte. As a girl Kate was unusually fair, beautiful features with a complexion to match. At age two years she had polio that deformed one of her legs. As an endearing person she was everyone's friend. I suspect that due to her frail condition Mom couldn't count on her as much as Mom counted on Berta. Nevertheless, she had chores and one was taking care of five year old me every Saturday afternoon. Routinely we were off to Merrisieled Park where she'd meet all her girl friends who had their younger siblings in tow and it was a weekly party! When I was seven, Kate and I went Christmas shopping together and that established a yearly precedent. When she married I imagined myself being humorous by giving her a rolling pin as was sometimes featured in the comics to clobber one's mate. In 1939 she and her high school sweetheart, Elmer Weinkauf, tied the knot in our family's parish church, Saint Joseph's. Elmer had employment as a chemist at the local Ball Band Plant and was an avid golfer. They had three children, two boys and one girl: Richard, Edward and Ruth. I was a frequent baby sitter for those nephews who were the forerunners of the next generation. Kate's transition was in 2008.

William (1-28-21): Some of my first recollections of Bill were his taking my wagon to the grocery store on Saturday mornings. Mom made out the marketing list and Bill attended to the rest. It was Bill who had a special understanding with Mom about his not wanting to eat chicken. It was an understood house rule that we ate what was served. Whatever aversion Bill had for chicken was something that Mom understood and Bill was served another dish. After Bill joined the army his letters home made Mom's week! I was so impressed having a brother who could write so descriptively about his worldly adventures. Bill was the middle of seven siblings. Sometimes I wonder how birth order affects siblings. Henry and two sisters were older than Bill, Herm, Chuck and I were younger. As a very bright young boy Bill somehow picked up the name, "Gabby." No doubt our parents tried to put a stop to it as Bill was deeply offended! Bill had a strong work ethic and an uncanny ability

to give a thorough explanation to any complicated question. During his career in the Air Force he held teaching assignments at the university level. For a time Bill provided government allotments that helped with expenses on the home front for Mom and me. In 1944, Bill and his Australian fiancée, Elizabeth Nell Payling, had a church wedding Down Under. They had four daughters and one son, Elizabeth, Moira, Christine, Joanna and William Jr. During his thirty two years with the military, the Air Force assignments stationed him and his family of five children in many locals, at home and abroad. Outdoor camping was a passion and they had all the necessary camping gear. Mother Nell ran a tight-ship as their entire family did extensive traveling, vacationing and camping. When I visited them in Las Vegas, Bill had a bookcase along the entire garage wall full of folded maps of places where they all had traveled. Bill retired with the rank of Chief Master Sergeant (CMS/AF). He had three years at Purdue and earned a Bachelor and Master's Degree simultaneously from Texas Christian College while stationed in Texas. Bill, a widower, resides in Florida near two of his daughters and has made frequent trips to Australia to visit daughter Moira and her family.

Herman (1-16-23): My first recollections of Herm are with him, Chuck and me, playing games at a card table in the dining room under a shelf that housed a clock that seemed to me to be made of gold. It was ten inches in height, enclosed with a glass dome and had a pendulum that rotated forever. All the deck of cards were well worn and it was an extra happy day when the monopoly game appeared, no doubt it was under a Christmas tree. Herm was habitually companionable as a youngster and as an adult. He was a realist, an optimist, a practical person who enjoyed all aspects of life from work to play. He taught me how to swim and how to handle a ball. I remember his enthusiasm for his first job as a teen pumping gas at the nearby gas station. His next job was house-sitting to answer the telephone for the doctor's night out. Herm had a love for all sports and became a popular guy on high school campus. His high school sweetheart, pretty, genuine and loving, Betty Ackenhusen, became his bride in 1943 at an East Coast Naval Station. Betty's parents had an untimely death and she and her brother were raised by her widowed aunt who was an office worker in the local plant, the Ball Band. Aunt Nettie was most caring and doted on Betty and her brother. Herman's Purdue degree was in Forestry. After a time among the trees, the isolationism of the forest, the yearning for nostalgia, they returned to their homestead with familiar old friends. Herm retired from office machinery sales work. I believe it was unfortunate for society that he didn't choose a teaching career as he would have been a fantastic high school science teacher and athletic coach! They had

two daughters, Nancy and Kathy. Herm was a widower for ten years before his death and frequently vacationed in California with me. We had many great times together! He was the prototype Optimist. His transition was in 2000.

Charles (6-28-24): Chuck is three years older and when I was six, and he nine, he frequently had the assignment to make sure I wasn't getting into mischief. He was always a caring big brother even when he was enticing me to help with one of his chores or his Cub Scout assignments. Chuck has always had a number of unusual streaks of uniqueness about him. He was strongly original, well centered, sensitive and most adaptable. I doubt that he ever took himself seriously except for his family. He created an art form with his ability to fracture the king's grammar and in so doing charmed the birds in flight!

At an early age he acquired the know-how-gift of making humor, and years later won the heart of Dorothy Goolie, a Mishawaka girl who graduated from Saint Joseph's Girl's Academy in South Bend. They married in her parish church, Saint Monica's. As a very smart girl she saw in Chuck a positive person who never spoke negatively about people (not even the nuns) and always found something of a humorous nature to share. Chuck quit high school to join the army and was wounded in The Battle of the Bulge. Chuck enjoyed his work as a truck driver for a local business and had no desire for an indoor job. Raising four children sometimes required tightening the purse strings, nevertheless, wife Dorothy believes she got the prize of the five brothers! They had four children; sons Tom, Mike, John and daughter Patricia. They reside in nearby Bremen at Lake of the Woods. They sold their home in town and settled into a cottage that Chuck had owned for some years and when renovating, he christened it: "That'ill do!"

My relationship with Herm and Chuck was always good. In the early years the three of us were frequently together. I recall huffing down Third Street to Saint Joe School and Mr. Homs, the insurance man, gave us a ride if his car wasn't overloaded with kids. There was an occasion or two when the three of us "snuck" down the back alley to smoke cigarette butts! I do believe we wondered why grown ups thought smoking was such a glamorous thing to do. And, there were some early mornings when the three of us had pillow fights and laughed hilariously!

Life's Ongoing Changes

The one area that I excelled in at Saint Joe was that of a sales person. There were endless raffles promoted by the nuns for anything and everything! Then there was my own ongoing endeavor to sell the most subscriptions to the local newspaper, The Mishawaka Enterprise. I was constantly the top seller and received recognition and a nice compensation. That lasted for several years and provided pocket money. At this same time, 1936, 37, 38, Alberta was earning her R. N. Degree at Saint Joseph School of Nursing in Mishawaka. Those student nurses were given ten monthly newsletters that they were expected to sell or pay for them. For three years I sold all those newsletters.

After Berta completed her schooling she bought a new bicycle for me. Besides having an identity with bicycles, I made stilts of varying heights. I was chided as the "stilt boy." My favorite stilts took me six feet off the ground and it was necessary to climb the weeping willow tree in the back yard to get on them. I hurried-home from school to get on my stilts and walk the main sidewalk in front of the house and have the kids from the nearby high school walk under my two long legs.

For several years Berta had the glamorous life of hostess with American Air Lines. In those early years of air travel registered nurses were aboard and their requirements were stringent. They were, literally, a hostess in those none pressurized DC 3 cabins. All twenty one passengers needed assurance from time to time, especially when those small planes fell into air pockets!

While history has shown that the DC 3 was one of the safest planes ever built, it nevertheless had some regrettable mishaps. Berta had a close call to death that she apparently shrugged. She was in New York on layover form her home base, Chicago, when she arrived early at the LaGuardia Air Field. The hostess scheduled for an earlier flight was running late and it was decided that she and Berta switch flights. The flight Berta was on landed safely, the other flight didn't.

My mark as a salesman came in 1943 when I wanted to earn pocket money. For a short time I got an after school job in a camera shop developing films.

That was fun but I found that I could earn more money selling photo coupons for photography studios. There were two such businesses in South Bend and I worked Saturdays, my own time. This was 1943 through 45, the war years. I usually made good money for those days, twenty or twenty five dollars for five or six hours of canvassing from door to door. The most lucrative days were when I found an area that had not been canvassed by other salesmen.

I rang thousands of doorbells in South Bend but didn't sell in town where I went to school. Meeting people at their front door was usually a pleasant encounter. "Hello! I'm representing the Goldberg Photo Studio on Washington Street, downtown, and we're having this special offer. -- Open folder showing three 8 by 10 portraits. -- For a short time and for as little as one dollar, you too can have a photo," etc. If the customer didn't like the Goldberg Studio, I was prepared and ripped out coupons for the Steinberg's Studio! The one dollar was my commission and the studios made their profit by selling additional photos.

Catherine had married and started a family of her own. This was 1944; Mom was fifty five years old. She had been a widow for two years. The only financial security that Pop left was the equity in the house. There were no social security benefits as that program was just beginning. Mom's skills were homemaker and child care provider. Bill's military allowance did much to provide for Mom and me. For a time, Mom took the smaller bedroom and rented her larger master room. Twice we had boarders, young chemists who worked with Kate's husband at the Ball Band.

I was earning enough money selling coupons to be extravagant on occasions. I acquired a nice wardrobe and I delighted Mom with presents. I frequently felt an energizing sensation that was partially due to the exoneration after ten miserable years at Saint Joe! In Mom's endeavor to adjust to being a widow she joined a church card playing group, called "The Sodality." They met twice a month. Mom loved all card games, especially bridge. Mom was a proud woman who had a lot of fun loving qualities that were sometimes suppressed when feeling insecure. At such times she exhibited signs of emphysema and a weakened heart condition, all very real. Mom was never a smoker.

Although my school years had a void from the wonders of reading, I did acquire vocabulary skills that helped me advance and I believe I developed strong intuitiveness. In this time frame, while in the 8th and 9th grades in the early 1940'S., I assumed I didn't have a wide range of choices for careers. Most employment required good reading and spelling skills of which I lacked. My favorite hobby was photography but I didn't allow myself to project where that might lead as a career considering my lack of those skills. At this early age I had resigned myself to a life career in sales.

The customary camera in those days was a box camera that required rolls of film that produced about ten or twelve exposures. I photographed scenes all over town, parks, favorite streets, public buildings, people, and learned how to make double exposures and time exposures as this was an era before flash bulbs. I converted a small area in the basement for developing my films. The dark room had to be pitch-dark with only a small red light providing lighting; any streak of regular light would ruin the process. There were two distinct operations: developing the roll of film to produce the negatives, and printing from the negatives onto special paper to produce the photograph. Both procedures required different chemicals. I acquired knowledge as a photographer and as a laboratory technician.

That basement area provided a valuable area for my many interests, particularly during the three years in attendance at the local high school. I created a recreation room by painting and decorating. I painted the walls, ceiling, floor, the old round oak dining table and chairs in an array of bright happy colors. I bought a junior size pool table and had my buddies in for games and soft drinks. I loved entertaining and fancied myself a very social person as I was also active in school organizations. I even

John H., Teacher Miss Davidson, Jerry, Charles R.

purchased colorful fiesta dinner ware to accommodate a spaghetti supper that Mom prepared and served after a hay ride that I organized. Farmers with their horses pulling hay wagons were for hire in my Hoosier State. We were sixteen teenagers wrapped in hay and snuggling together as we all went trumping through the country corn fields during a bracing October evening singing spirited songs.

I dated different girls as I enjoyed the social life, but I never entertained a romantic entanglement. I loved dancing and I was good at jitterbugging as that was the craze. During my freshman year I went out for football and played right end and on the track team I ran the 880. During my second and third year I preferred the social life at the corner drug store instead of sports. I believe I was well liked by fellow students and teachers although I did feel academically handicapped, but maintained passing grades.

When I reflect on those days, as a psychology buff and former teacher, I surmise that some decisions I made back them were to compensate for the rejection I experienced at Saint Joe. One regretful effort was having been a ring leader in forming an exclusive social club with limited membership of fifteen or twenty. I cruised the school's campus, flaunting the club's uniquely designed jacket to exhibit my worth. Today, I couldn't sanction such exclusiveness in a public school of any size, and this high school had over eleven hundred students. The year book from Mishawaka High School is titled the *Miskadeed*. Several such books are favorites in my library as I thoroughly enjoyed reminiscing about the academic training and the life that school provided. After ten painful years in elementary school, this high school with its wonderful teaching staff was indeed a blessing. My three wonderful years at Mishawaka High School were indeed a blessing!

Downtown Mishawaka, Indiana, 1940, a few blocks from St. Joe, One and a half mile from home.

Mishawaka High School , Three short blocks from home.

Moving On

September '45 through May '46, my junior year in high school and my last year at home was an eventful period! Berta had married and had baby Mary. When husband Bill was drafted Berta and Mary came home for a time. For two years I was assigned the General Course in high school and made passing grades! My reading had improved a little but my spelling was an abomination. Papers were returned to me with misspelled words underlined that resembled a score board for ticktacktoe.

During this summer of '45, weeks before my eighteenth birthday, I was trifling, and ultimately flirting, with a nice looking twenty five year old while sipping a coke at the Walgreens Drug Store in the adjacent town. The mirrors behind the counter that we both confronted served as our introduction. There were two blushing faces reflecting in that mirror; I could feel my face turning scarlet with the passing moments. The long time smiles that we had for one another conveyed the message: "I want to know you!" I was so eager for contact that I spotted a booth and nodded to him that we should move there. He acknowledged with an ever so bright smile as I assessed the moment. I was pleased that he matched my six foot height. He seemed quite reserved and introduced himself as I rattled off some mundane observation. His name was Todd. I soon felt the warmth that Todd radiated as he inquired about my schooling, family and interests. The resonance of his kind voice and masculine demeanor were assurance that I'd like him.

I was overwrought with excitement/anticipation when our knees met and maintained a strong pressure! We talked of many things except the feeling of exhilaration running through my loin. There were two sources of communication going on, one above and another below the table. The suspenseful moments were electrifying flurry that was soul-stirring! We agreed to meet the following afternoon. That night I made passionate love to my pillow pretending it was Todd. At two 0'clock the following day those incredible Walgreen mirrors welcomed us! Had there not been any salutation, our togetherness would have completed the moment. Later that day we were in his living quarters and there was no pretending, no will-o'-the-wisp longings. We were experiencing a real life-living-force, a wondrous happening!

During the following year this secret affair had more than just romantic couplings. With friendship I learned that Todd was an army officer who had recently received an honorable discharge and was now connected in the academic world. We kept in touch until his transition, for some thirty years. In the early sixties we attended a football game together at the Los Angeles Coliseum. We had choice seats on the 50 yard line. I find it difficult to forget seeing one player being carried off the field while spitting out a mouthful of broken teeth. Todd and I also shared many cheerful memories besides that sad event.

My friendship with Todd was an acknowledgement of who I am! I recall my feelings of wanting to express great exuberance! Music was most exhilarating! I could sing every song being played on the hit parade and Mom's recordings of the Strauss' waltzes and ballet music were total ecstasy! When I was home alone I had a compulsion to throw myself into all forms of dance without any resistance! My body jived with jitterbug music and it glided smoothly to ballet music until I twirled and pirouetted from room to room with utter exhaustion! I was experiencing what I had long believed would be the unraveling of a happy fate to come.

A major concern was wondering what my life would be like after my senior year? With my academic record I wouldn't be going off to college. Of course Mom would be happy if I found a local job and lived at home. I found comfort in realizing that Mom would have Kate and Chuck living nearby. Chuck was home from the war and engaged to be married and had a local job. My genes were reason enough to locate to a cosmopolitan city where I'd find alliance with like minded people and make friends. I also felt that the only type job I'd be suited for would be in the world of commercial sales.

 I assumed that if I were a salesman I'd represent some big company selling quality merchandise. I applied prematurely and had an offer from Cluett & Peabody, a Chicago firm, to work my way up to salesman by beginning as an office boy. I managed to persuade Mom into letting me move to Chicago, a distance of a hundred miles, where I could finish my senior year while working for Cluett & Peabody. I would go to Lake View Evening High and I'd be living near Berta and Bill as they planned to be living there while Bill took a residency in surgery.

My leaving home was a difficult decision for Mom. She understood that I was looking to map a life course/career that would make me happy. I sometimes wonder if she wasn't aware of my sexual proclivities; mothers often know. She knew I liked big city life and that in a year after graduation I would want to relocate. Mom talked about the day when I'd leave, and at such time she'd sell the house and make living conditions elsewhere, which all came to pass with the decision that I could take the job with Cluett & Peabody. Had I stayed in Mishawaka I would have graduated in June, 1947, three months before my twentieth birthday.

Mom did sell the house after I left home. Mom was fifty eight years old and her children were beginning their families. Mom looked into several living arrangements before deciding to take employment as a companion to an elderly woman, the mother of a Notre Dame Professor. Mom enjoyed being a member of that family for a few years before settling into her own apartment. In her declining years Mom made her home with daughter Kate and wintered with me.

The Lake at the University of Notre Dame – Taken on one of my many hikes there.

Playwrights and producers

Maturing

For over a year I was on my own, working, getting that diploma was part of my maturing experience. The other part was this "entire society" that I knew I belonged to, and I wanted to know some of those counterparts. In the late 1940s big cities could be more amenable to Gays than towns with provincial attitudes. As for adhering to legislation against Gays, I learned at Saint Joe that city ordinances, like some church laws, are frequently made for undo control. Men having political clout are sometimes mistaken for being moral persons who will frequently instigate laws for the sake of their own political agenda, thus, corruption.

Finding suitable rentals after the war in any large city was next to impossible. In Chicago I found a one room apartment for Berta, Bill and Mary and an even smaller one for myself in the same building. We considered ourselves lucky with such living conditions even with a community bathroom down the hall. In spite of such conditions, I knew I did the right thing by leaving my homestead. I had to grow up. There was this whole part of society that I needed to understand.

My job as office boy paid a pittance and didn't begin to cover bare living expenses; I found another job behind a lunch counter and started viewing life from a different perspective. I knew I wanted more education whether it included sales work or something else. I had some talent for drawing and art and I knew I was gaining confidence in all aspects of maturity.

There were a few weekends when Todd came to Chicago to see me and other friends. We met at the Gay Bar in the Sherman Hotel in the downtown Loop Area. My education regarding Gay life was expanding and in the late 1940s that was something important to understand and have one's guard up. In those days it wasn't permissible for Gays to be themselves. Frequently Gays had to live out their entire lives disguised to be straight when seeking employment, housing and even relating with family. I never came out to family regarding my Gay gene. Gays wanting to meet other Gays could go to Gay bars, but there was always a chance that it might be raided and you'd be hauled away in a paddy wagon. That meant either sitting in jail or posting bail-money, and the entire ball of wax. Some local governments were corrupt and this was one way to obtain easy money. Fortunately I never got into any legal or scandalous messes during my conservative escapades.

For a time I had a couple of short romances. One weekend I met vacationing 28 year old Ben from San Antonio, Texas. We got fairly well acquainted in a short time and then he left without a trace. I was most disappointed. Several weeks passed when a man came to the lunch counter where I worked. Once he knew my name he introduced himself as being from the Over the Rainbow Missing Person's Bureau, and said he had a message for me. It was from Ben! He wanted me to phone him. I did and soon after Ben flew to Chicago to see me.

He knew I wanted more schooling and encouraged me to enroll in a college where he taught. It was understood that I'd find a part time job and enroll in several classes. I was able to save a few dollars as Ben bought my train ticket to Texas.

Ben met me at the train station in San Antonio. Instead of going to his place as he originally planned, he helped me locate a rooming house near the college. After several days of searching I began to realize there were no part time jobs for students. There was an over abundance of inexpensive local laborers. I was experiencing a high degree of frustration as I had parted with some limited cash for rooming and tuition. About the third day Ben confessed that he and his partner of some years decided to reconcile and there would be no further relation between us. He apologized.

I realized I was on the wrong path and left San Antonio while I still had bus fair to get to Los Angeles. I was searching for direction and decided to locate an art school in Los Angeles. I would enroll and I'd manage! Armed with little more than self confidence, I began feeling good about myself and knew that this time I was on the right path. Horace Greeley's admonition, "Go West, young man," was right for me!

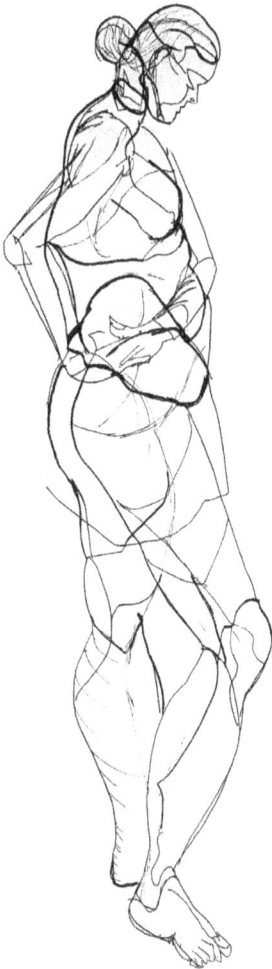

Los Angeles and Jepson Art Institute

I arrived in Los Angeles with two dollars in my pocket and headed for Western Union where I wired brother Henry to send me twenty five dollars. With that in hand I located a nice enough boarding house near Hollywood. It took several days before Thrifty Drug Stores hired me to work behind one of their soda fountains. In good time I met people and got oriented to the terrain. This was 1948, the Pasadena Freeway was the only freeway in that sprawled out metropolis of what appeared to be many villages of varying sizes. Sometime later I was working behind the counter at the popular Dolores Drive-In on the celebrated trendy Sunset Strip, a noted scene back then. It boasted of night clubs and restaurants where celebrities were touted and ballyhooed about in the tabloids. This was the time after the war when people were spending money freely. Manufactured goods were not plentiful in stores. Working for wages and tips could be lucrative. Some displaced European royalty took jobs as chamber maids for the tips received. Dolores Drive-In operated from noon until two a.m. The camaraderie of fellow workers was always upbeat as they formed a group of goal oriented fellows including some who were striving to make their mark in the movie industry.

Dolores' menu was limited to a few items, but everything was uncommonly special. Hamburgers were the main attraction with their highly touted Dolores sauce. Among the frequent celebrities in the news was the gangster, Mickey Cohen, who maintained his headquarters directly across the street. Frequent phone orders from that center of operations for deliveries to their front door were most welcomed as they were rewarded generously. The adjacent neighborhood below The Strip was composed of modest bungalows, perhaps fifteen or twenty years old and that is where I found living quarters for several months. The structure I lived in had four or five small living quarters and the occupants shared a community kitchen. Such conditions suited me as I could walk to work and save to buy a car which was essential in that metropolis.

After several months I bought a 1937 Dodge Coupe, my first car. For some time I had been creating an art portfolio to present to several art schools as I was looking for a tuition free scholarship. I remember one drawing in particular. It was my rendition of the beautiful actress, Olivia de Havilland, appearing not very glamorous in a terrifying scene from the movie, Snake Pit. I had to chuckle whenever I looked at that drawing because it reminded to me of a few nuns that I had at Saint Joe.

I didn't find a commercial art school but was accepted at the Jepson Art Institute. In exchange for tuition I pushed a broom after classes five afternoons a week. Enrollment at Jepson's was comprised mostly of GI students with acclaimed artist/instructors, Francis De Erdely, Rico Lebrun, Milly Rocque, William Brice, Roger Hollenbeck, Guy McCoy, Howard Warshaw and others. Classes were designed with objectives: Drawing towards composition, Design and Color towards Advertising Art, Figure Drawing towards Drawing Research and Art History, Silk Screen Design toward Lithography, Figure Drawing towards Magazine Illustrations. It was the perfect school for me! I loved being there!

Without intervention from anyone, my application for a one room apartment with full kitchen was accepted. Such vacancies were indeed difficult to come by in 1949. I managed to establish a good rapport with the middle aged woman manager by making frequent enquiries. The three story well built building was probably built some 15 years earlier and all units in this elevator building had pull down Murphy beds that folded and swung into a closet. The units were sparsely furnished. Garages were not provided, so cars lined the adjacent streets. The location of this apartment structure and the Jepson Art Institute were in the city's Wilshire district, near 7th St. and Hoover. I often worked a few hours weekdays but my main hours for Dolores Drive-In were Friday evenings and long hours on weekends. Mom came for a week's stay and we had a lovely visit between my schooling and working. I was meeting interesting people at school and learning skills for a carrier in the field of art. My horizons were so much greater here than they would have been had I stayed in Mishawaka. I was experiencing a field of positive energy. Life was good!

My world at age 21 in 1948 was drastically different from Henry's world when he was 21 in 1936-37. Henry, at 21 was forging ahead academically in times of inordinate economic slowdown. My progress at age 21 in 1948 had been academically compromised and I was progressing at a slower rate in a thriving economy.

At age 25 in 1940, Henry enrolled in a government sponsored program, Civilian Pilot Training. After ten hours of flight instruction he was washed out due to landing the craft. He wrote, "Every time I made a landing I leveled off about six feet in the air." Poor depth perception was his fate. When Herman entered the service he had high hopes to earn "wings." He was rejected for flight training due to some eye deficiency. None of my siblings had pilot license although Bill's career was in the Air Force. I believe I was the only sibling who started wearing eye glasses in my teens.

Berta, Henry and Herman circa 1938
Mary and Barbara, daughters of Berta;
Nancy, daughter of Herman

Mary

Barbara

Nancy

Dr. Bob & Florence

"I have a friend that I'd like you to meet."

Professor Kelly was a frequent customer at Dolores. He was a retired art teacher from Columbia U. in New York. When he learned that I was going to Jepson Art Institute, he wanted to know more about me. His friend that he thought I'd enjoy knowing was also an artist. I acknowledged the invitation and explained that right then I had a busy schedule. I was adjusting to several changes; I had purchased a car and I was transferring to Dolores' other location at La Cienega and Wilshire where I'd work in the dining room several evenings a week and on weekends; I was getting acclimated to new quarters in a new neighborhood, and was learning the clean up chores following classes at Jepson.

Weeks later Kelly contacted me and we visited his friend, Dr. Robert Kennicott. Doctor Bob was most hospitable. His graciousness was second only to his good looks. I assumed that he was probably around forty years of age and I immediately liked his enthusiasm, his combination of manliness and sensitivity. The three of us spent the greater part of the evening in his studio viewing his art work. I liked the aroma, the smell of paints and there were paintings on all walls and paintings neatly stacked in bins. I was in awe of his talent, his output! He worked in all medias, oils, watercolors, waxes and he did sculpting and wood carving. I fantasized being intimate with him when he said he'd like to paint a portrait of me.

The following eighteen months were among the happiest days of my life. As an art student I would be acquiring skills that would put me in good stance for a carrier in the art world. Several times a week I was with Bob and our relationship grew. I learned that he had recently been Chief of Staff at his Good Samaritan Hospital, and during the war years he headed up the local medical chapter of the American Red Cross. After he had known me several months he was calling me, "his ward". Mom met him during her visit and they related well. Both enjoyed a good sense of humor and both had my interest at heart. I was well received by his associates and friends.

As my mentor and physician, Dr. Bob diagnosed my reading handicap as a form of dyslexia that could be corrected. He worked with me and gave me reassurance that I had much hidden potential and innate intelligence that I could succeed at whatever I wished. In time I met his friend and patient, Florence Cuningham, a middle aged spinster, elocutionist, from New England, who located to Beverly Hills where she worked for the motion picture industry, particularly for Howard Hughes. I saw her for lessons and she and Bob practically turned my world upside down. Her teaching instruments included poetry cards with words underlined. I would repeat these words many times to associate the vowels sounds. It was a deliberate effort to see the vowels and hear the sounds. She always invited me to compose myself before a lesson began to lessen any stress or anxiety that I might have. As I attended to my homework assignments, the phonics cards and work sheets to learn spelling, I gained self confidence. In time I was remembering how to spell and I gained fluency in reading! My progress was considerable! Dr. Bob did not make disparaging remarks about the nun teachers. Of course, I credit my father for his undying devotion to helping me nightly, primarily with sight vocabulary, for five years! Back then I learned enough to squeeze by. I do suspect there was some sort of chemical imbalance that caused learning interference during childhood, along with a dislike for the nuns and what was being taught about religion, including partnership with one's own sex.

Perhaps in time biological research will have an explanation regarding the varying factors that hindered my ability to learn reading during those grade school days. What contributed to the attention deficit?

How could the gene factor affect reading, or the effects of harsh/cruel discipline on a child with a gay gene? What is known of the Gay gene in the "birth order" in families? My lore may help research. Regarding analysis at some point, it should be noted that while great strides in reading were made during my twenties, I never arrived at being the one hundred percent proficiency expert reader I admired and aspired. It is acknowledged that there are numerous levels of reading efficiency. I suspect that the component to becoming a gifted reader is best acquired in sequence to learning reading at an early age.

Reading with Dr. Bob

A holiday visit with Florence

Have you ever rightly considered what the mere ability to read means? That it is the key which admits us to the whole world of thought and fancy and imagination? To the company of saint and sage, of the wisest and the wittiest at their wisest and wittiest moment? That it enables us to see with the keenest eyes, hear with the finest ears, and listen to the sweetest voices of all times?

James Russell Lowell

The Navy – Meeting Mike – The Mine Disaster

In the spring of 1950 the Korean War escalated to where the military draft was reinstated. I would be drafted! Being an art student at Jepson's Fine Art Institute didn't qualify for military exemption. It had occurred to me to simply declare that I was homosexual and I'd be exempt from military duty. For years I had sought for this career direction and had experienced only 16 months, and at this date to give it all up! Oh! The pain, the depression! I would be 23 years old in September. Many in my age bracket were winding down their career preparation and I was just beginning! Going into the military would be another deferment in preparation for a career. Moreover, I wondered what assignment I would have in either the army or the navy. That was a big concern! No matter what branch of service I'd go into, I would be given aptitude tests. All such tests used paper, pencil and required reading. My conditioning at St. Joe was such that I knew I'd freak out as I always did when testing! I had developed self confidence in some areas but lacked assurance with testing that required reading. Granted, my reading had improved as of recent, but still, testing?

I could have been a conscientious objector. The honesty behind such rationale would not be that I could continue art school, but that I honestly abhor killing. I had often reflected about the thousands of battlefields in the history of the world with dead soldiers strewn all about. For history's many wars the killings of "us versus them" are in reality, in a way, our leaders versus their leaders and vice versa. So many young men, some with their heads blown off, died at the hands of someone who pulled a trigger or threw a spear or a grenade while longing to be held and caressed by the very likes of the person he killed. The sweet taste of being a loving human marveling at life's mysteries while caressing another like minded soul was hijacked for a premature death in a war zone! Ask a mother what she would choose if the choice had to be between having a dead loving straight son or a living loving Gay son? Having a deferment in 1950 because one was homosexual carried an unmentionable ugly stigma.

My decision was discussed with Dr. Bob. Certainly he was a patriot having headed up the American Red Cross in Los Angeles during the war years. I was mindful of four older brothers who served honorably; and Chuck was wounded in the Battle of the Bulge. Weighing in on this heart rendering decision was that my parents adopted the United States over their birth country, Holland.

My personal possessions were stored at Dr. Bob's. I spent several hours at the outdoor incinerator burning dozens of drawing tablets that represented my work for the past sixteen months. Just before finalizing what was a downcast chore, I reached into the dancing flames and pulled out the last tablet. From that I tore out a few sheets for mementos sake. Some years later I framed four line drawings as they represented a happy time in my life.

So in June 1950 I began serving four years in the U. S. Navy. After boot camp in San Diego I was assigned to the deck crew aboard the destroyer, Harry E. Hubbard. My combat station was being part of a crew handling artillery shells that fed a 25 millimeter machine. There were frequent nights when my shipmates and I fired ammunition upon Korean shores. For several months I followed daytime orders from a boatswain to paint or chip paint or cleanup whatever. If I had ever contemplated committing suicide this would have been the time. After a couple of months I was transferred to the Supply Division. I took refrigerator supplies from the walk in freezers up to the galley and kept some inventory. Destroyers were often referred to as "tin cans." My tin can was regularly home based in San Diego after several months duty at sea.

Jerry & Mike in Hawaii at Don the Beach Comber

On June 12, 1951, a sister destroyer in our taskforce, the USS Walke, cruising just ahead of us hit a mine! A huge hole was torn in the ship's hull and brought death to men inside that compartment. Horrifying! That part of the ship took on gushing water and hatches leading to that compartment were closed! There were volunteers from the Hubbard who attended to some impending needs concerning the dead sailors who died so wretchedly. The following day the USS Walke went listing off to a dry dock in Japan. How sad it is that such warring casualties throughout the ages are soon forgotten unless they involve our own loved ones. The terror of war!

I was grateful that my reading ability had improved as I read unremittingly while patrolling with the Taskforce. Reading short stories became a favorite past time. Sherwood Anderson's Winesburg Ohio became a favorite. I reread those stories several times enjoying the realism and intrigue and his style of writing. I enjoyed writing and receiving letters; Bob always included a list of my misspelled words. He also reminded me that I had a home whenever the ship was home based. There were a number of visits to Japanese ports,

Sasebo, Yokohama, and Yokosuka. There was a onetime visit to Hong Kong and frequent trips to Pearl Harbor.

My best friend aboard ship was Mike Nissen, the ship's personnel man who occupied the ship's office adjacent to my storekeeper's office. Mike and I made several voyages to Japan on this tin-can. The usual liberty in any foreign port was souvenir shopping for those back home. For some sailors it was finding a whore house to their liking. For Berta, I repeatedly purchased bolt after bolt of raw silk! Berta made clothes for herself and her children and draperies for their rented house in Chicago. When they moved she took the draperies with her and made more clothes. Such was their economy as Bill finalized his residency in lung surgery.

While exploring foreign Yokosuka, Mike and I located a small quaint tea room that lit up our imagination. It was named, The New Saint Louis. The menu was limited to pastries, coffee, tea and liqueur. There were several small rooms, unpretentious, but equipped stereophonically for the guest to make their selection from a large library of classical music, many operas. Music by Puccini and Verdi never sounded more beautiful! We made friends with the owners, a most pleasant middle aged couple, and there were a few small gift exchanges. An assortment of seeds of flowers and vegetables that I purchased in California was a gift to them. I was so taken with the New Saint Louis that I wondered if I might have my own such opera salon serving liqueurs, back in Los Angeles.

A most memorable day was spent in the captivating historic city of Kamakura where we explored the inside of their enormous bronze statue of Buddha. It was springtime and the tree lined sidewalks had cherry blossoms casting sweet scents of efflorescence all about. Buddha was over forty feet in height and was cast in the thirteen century. We visited the nearby national art museum that held treasures of priceless beauty and antiquity. The fondest purchase in my life was made in Kamakura's gift shop. It is a seventeen inch ceramic statue of a warrior of long ago. The face is distinctly Chinese, he is wearing an almond colored glazed garment and both arms are bent at the elbow, one arm stretched forward, the other arm reaches upward. I have reason to believe that it is authentic, and probably has an intriguing history. For a time I misappropriated his sex and called him Ethel. Since I've learned that Ethel was indeed a warrior, and now he is Edwin.

Mike, like Dr. Bob, had a notable influence on me although their backgrounds were entirely different. Dr. Bob came from an affluent background as his father was an attorney in St. Paul, Minnesota, his maternal grandfather Helm, was a clerk of the Supreme Court in St. Paul, and the naturalist Kennicott, for whom the Alaska copper mines are named was his great uncle.

Mike was born in an Iowa town of one hundred. His mother died when he was three and his father became the town's drunk. Mike was often abandoned, shuffled about, and ultimately made his home with the town's telephone/ switchboard operator whom he called Aunt Annie. He slept on a cot in the kitchen and as a child found small jobs including dish washer in a small café. He was motivated to do well in school and after two years of college he was eligible to teach. It was in a small rural one room school house where he developed his love for teaching. Alone, he conducted cross age education classes with grades first through eighth. The conditions were most primitive with outside toilets and drinking water brought from home. Before joining the Navy he had three years of college and two years teaching experience.

One weekend when I was going to Bob's I invited Mike to join me. My good friend Bill would be visiting there; on occasions Bill had joshed: "Bring me a sailor boy!" The previous year Bill had lost his partner of several years to cancer and was still adjusting to being alone. Bill and Mike no sooner met when sparks lit up the evening sky like fireflies! They seemed so alike in stature, interests and temperament that the age difference of ten years didn't make any difference to either. After they retired to the guest room, it was Bob who made a bouquet of orange blossoms and attached it to their bedroom door. I'm told that magical violins played throughout the night. The bright light lasted some 48 years until Bill's death.

I surely missed Mike when he left the ship to join the admiral's staff in San Diego. When he was discharged he completed college and taught in the Inglewood School District. Eventually we were both taking classes together at State and USC. After some years of teaching he went into administration, vice principal to principal to curriculum director for the district. The highly esteemed training school at UCLA arranged for him to take a leave of absence from Inglewood so he could assist them with his expertise, wisdom and judgment. After being in the education field for thirty years he retired and took a job with the teamster union in Long Beach and can say that most jobs are less stressful than that in the field of education. Mike and I talk daily via phone and usually exchange a few zingers. We each think we can out zing the other.

Recollecting life aboard ship at sea brought about memories for Mike as he recalled a high degree of sexual energy, or homoeroticism is another word for it. His personnel office, the ship's office, was often invaded after evening chow with crew members just wanting to hangout. All kinds of talk and sometimes playful jesters and innuendoes, no subjects barred. There was a tall well built married guy from the engineering department who took a particular shine to Mike. During his frequent visits he'd physically picked up all 125 pounds of

Mike while he took possession of the chair for himself and had Mike sitting on his lap. There was no fondling although that would have been the next step for either guy to initiate. Mike can recall many incidences of sexual energy. All personnel had their military records on file in his office and that was their entry. Mike was Mr. Popularity of the Harry E. Hubbard. He could write a best seller about horny sailors at sea while bombarding Korean shores at night.

My encounters with crew members were minimized as I felt withdrawn much of the time. My focus was always away from the Navy. A day didn't go by that I hadn't longed for my former life as a civilian attending art school. In my attempt to be part of the crew I contributed an article to the ship's biweekly news letter. The salutation was, "Dear Mom," supposedly a letter home that focused on the ship's activities of the recent weeks. I especially enjoyed writing about my impressions when visiting foreign ports and how the customs differed from those back home. I did surprise myself for having such thriving nerve to write when I was such a poor speller! I believe my inspiration to write came from the recent reading of short stories. I did use the dictionary and I was assured that someone would proof read my articles.

My free weekends and annual leaves were spent at Bob's. I did fly back to family in Indiana a few times. Weekend passes usually ran from 4 PM Friday to 7 am Mondays. I'd get to Los Angeles by hitching a ride with someone or taking a greyhound bus. During the last year I drove my 1937 Dodge as parking lots were available for servicemen. There were occasions when I'd fly back to San Diego late Sunday evening as we lived near the Los Angeles Airport. Every time I flew I ran into shipmate Carver from the gunnery department. He was about forty years of age, a career man who was Mr. Sunshine to everyone aboard ship. We became quite friendly and he learned about Dr. Bob and I learned about his special boy friend of many years. Interesting though, while we knew intuitively the other's sexual proclivity, neither of us felt free to acknowledge our identity as such.

Dr. Bob in his studio

College and Living with Dr. Bob

In the spring of 1954 I received an honorable discharge. Once again I felt relieved and liberated! I had the GI bill and enrolled at Los Angeles Junior College. I was there for two years, two years at L. A. State for a bachelor degree and two years at USC earning a Master's Degree and entertaining the idea of working for a PhD in psychology. During these six years I made my home with Dr. Bob and his mother in the Baldwin Hills. Bob's mother, Maude Helm Kennicott, was a small boned fragile lady in her nineties and required bed rest. She would leave her room with walker for short exercises, or to "sit down there," and for 6 PM dinner in the dining room. Her breakfast was served as she sat up in bed. By the bedroom windows was a Duncan Phyfe table with hinged leaves that pulled up and accommodated Bob with the Los Angeles Morning Times that he read aloud. I was there at our

Dr. Bob with his whimsical Songbird painting

customary morning breakfast table with Bob, and Mrs. K. until her death in '58. My assignment was to be home by 3:30 when the house keeper/nurse/cook left. It was important that Mrs. K. not be left alone.

A six foot slender frame with a kind face might well describe Bob's appearance. On a couple occasions he was mistaken for the actor, Joseph Cotton. He was an avid reader. A few of his favorite writers were, Henry James, Andre Gide and Christopher Isherwood. Bob had an abounding energy level that was shared between his medical practice, his world of art and his gardening. Sometimes after a busy day at the office he read the electrocardiograms in bed. In those days cardiograms were on rolls of paper about three inches wide and they might be four or five feet in length. In addition to having a secretary he had a laboratory technician and a clientele ranging from poor to very wealthy. His temper could be shortened by someone's constant complaints. There was a particular wealthy dowager who unloaded once too often as far as Dr. Bob was concerned, and he said: "There's nothing wrong with you, Anna, that wouldn't be cured if you got down on your knees and scrubbed your own kitchen floor!" Needless to say that was the last time the good doctor made a house call to Anna's stately home in that exclusive district.

One might describe Dr. Bob as a self assured person with many corners. He was a dedicated doer for many causes he believed in, medicine, blood bank, art, institutes for learning, and individuals. For many years he championed me as I was "his ward" while I was in the service and in college.

Altar boy with comics, circa 1943

Going back to 1952 & 53, when I was in the Navy, I spent my liberty at home with Dr. Bob and his mother. That was the era when McCarthyism was flourishing along with J. Edgar Hoover's thrust on Communism. Perhaps that era of American history is best forgotten. It lasted long enough to ruin the lives and careers of many talented good people who belonged to, or suspected of belonging to, the Communist Party. A family that Bob was fond of was suspected of having attended such meetings and consequently was blackballed and suspended by the Hollywood studios. I was with Bob during a Christmas Season when we delivered a large basket of groceries from Balzar's Market. Delivering was not a simple procedure as homes were being spied upon. I was the "lookout" as Bob patrolled the area for five minutes before parking and delivering the groceries.

On a number of occasions Dr. Bob invited me to join him at the lunchroom in the Good Samaritan Hospital. He took pride in introducing me, "his ward," to his colleagues. Bob was well liked and highly respected by the hospital staff. I made lifelong friends with several of his friends. Dr. Sidney Burnap, a surgeon, and wife Margaret wanted me to have a family heirloom, a desk that he received from his mother at his graduation and used in his office for 25 years of medical practice in New York State, and 25 years in Los Angeles. I am using the desk as I write.

Bob's neighbor, Madolyn Hanley, and he each owned adjacent lots next to their homes. Bob cultivated a garden with a variety of plants. Bringing plants home from Howard's Nursery was almost a solemn occasion. It was as if plants and God were one and the same. Bob liked maneuvering a hand held power plow that had a six foot handle. The soil was aerated before planting anew. One of his garden specialties was growing carnations that provided a daily fresh boutonniere. His Fuerte avocados were distinctively ambrosial. To die for!

The year 1954 was when Bob traded-in his classic black Buick for a Ford Station Wagon. Bob needed transportation for the larger paintings he was doing. Some years back he had already established himself as a fine painter. In 1939 he received prominent recognition for a nude oil painting shown in the San Francisco International Exhibit. It was his resourcefulness, his acumen, to explore new frontiers in the world of painting and the creative arts. He and artist friend Mabel Alvarez joined the stimulating art classes conducted by Sister Corita at Immaculate Heart College in Hollywood.

Among Sister Corita's varied homework assignments was one that I have reckoned with. It was to observe an ordinary pencil and write twenty objective statements about it. She made some assignments that required using a "finder." A finder can be quickly made from paper, 3 x 5 or 8 x 8, any size, with the inside removed to make a frame. The purpose of the frame was to search for designs, shapes, thus a finder. Bob favored the photos that appeared in the newspaper sports section because they usually required exaggerated body composition. He'd turn the newspaper sideways and upside down using the finder in search of exceptional designs. I have a 2 ½ x 4 foot painting that used a 4 x 5 inch news paper photo. The photo was of the Pope standing on his balcony in the Vatican. The shapes in the painting suggest a flower cart with potted plants; so, I call the painting, "The Pope as a Pot." The painting was made with a wax media.

There were no dull days living with Bob. His friends were accomplished, well informed people that contributed to society and to discussions about current events, art, religion, books and life. Bob was not politically or religiously committed. He was an independent and an agnostic. His world was medicine and caring for patients, the prominent wealthy and many poor, providing for his mother, gardening in the "South Forty" for flowers and vegetables, and his consuming love for painting and sketching, producing numerous works of art that were exhibited or just another exercise that he fancied.

While Dr. Bob identified himself as an agnostic, he was very much a humanitarian. By the late 1950 he became dedicated to Sister Corita's Immaculate Heart of Mary order with their ardent devotion to teaching. At this time the sisters began a building fund for expansion. There were a number of

Sunday afternoon meetings to rally the cause. A professional organization that specializes in raising money became engaged. Occasionally I joined Bob at the college as he became involved as a dominate contributor. One Sunday I was in the audience when a paid professional made a statement contrasting Catholic education to Protestant education. Sister Corita considered the observation inappropriate and immediately corrected him by assuring the audience that there were many non Catholics interested in contributing to their building fund. She had indeed created a following!

Until I started teaching in the fall of 1960, I was a full time student at USC. As a major in Education and a minor in psychology I took many courses in psychology. I was interested in courses dealing with human sexuality. As a thirty year old living with Dr. Bob I didn't recall being unduly troubled in formative years about my sexuality to the degree of not liking myself. The study of psychology can illustrate how complicated people's sexual proclivities can be. Self loathing and suicide are common among young Gays in our culture. Ever since I can remember I knew I was different and people were going to think about me what they wanted. So, I knew I should always conduct myself with a positive attitude and self assurance. At no time was I confronted for having a Gay gene.

Customizing my designer's driveway – a labor of love

My sexual orientation was a concern that I kept to myself. As a thirty year old student reflecting on those days at Saint Joe, I was determined back then, not to allow any embarrassing learning experiences to pull me down. My self defense in those years was to reject what I found offensive. I especially didn't relate with those nuns and their "take on life, sin and religion." They were so repugnant, so disagreeable for me that I learned how to reject, how to cope with adversity. The psych classes helped me realize that I might have had a worse fate other than having a dyslexic challenge, and the coping with pressure when having a pencil in hand and facing a test paper.

When vacation time permitted I took on projects around the house. As part of landscaping the hillside garden I developed skills with cement. I liked mixing my own mortar in a trough and laying cement blocks or bricks. There was nothing wrong with the driveway from the street to the garage, perhaps 16 x 22 feet, but I envisioned something with more character. I broke up the existing driveway with a sledge hammer and replaced it with red bricks in a herring bone design. It was truly a "signature job" as there wasn't another like it! Working with cement became a passion with me. I was creating! I tackled similar projects in most real estate that I owned. I had something in common with Winston Churchill; we were both masons!

In the summer of 1955, Dr. Bob and I vacationed to New Orleans and Alberta's home in Pikeville, Kentucky. Berta's husband, Bill Hambley, was a lung surgeon and in the mid 1960'S he also became mayor of that coal mining community. Our visit predated the ticker-tape parade of 1987 celebrating a monumental event. From 1960 thru '67 Bill made trips to Washington for federal aid to reroute the river through the mountains in his Appalachian town; from 1967 through '87 there was ongoing construction. Dr. Bob and I were there before the big transformation of Pikeville into the culture center that it became. The two physicians and Berta related beautifully as they had met previously at Bob's home while I was at sea. This was a two week vacation away from our Los Angeles home. I spent one week in Pikeville and one week in Mishawaka visiting Mom and family. Bob spent two weeks in Pikeville painting portraits of Berta and Bill as well as their house. We had the "red carpet treatment!"

Plans regarding my future living conditions had been discussed two years before the summer of 1960. When I did move, Bob's close friend, Kay Campbell, a widow, had built a house where he had his South Forty Garden. Having my own living quarters meant I was able to have family for prolonged visits and I would see more of my peers. Bob and Kay spent their days painting and at cocktail time they brought out their day's work and critiqued each other's labor of love. Bob died in 1983 at age 91. He enjoyed a most productive life. I believe it was unfortunate that he never engaged an agent to promote his work as he received numerous favorable reviews from critics.

A good laugh, Dr. Bob and Mom, 1949

Dr. Bob, Mom and Jerry – Masters USC, 1959

A Range of Paintings

Jerry in Red Jacket
24x29 Oil 1952

Boy with Shell
20x24 Oil
Circa 1935

Water Color 18 x 24
Mythology 1954

Easter Parade
Oil 24X36
Circa 1979

Jerry in Yellow
Jacket 10x12
Oil 1954

50

Jerry Shades of Brown
Oil – 1957 18x20

Sister Corita Kent & the Archbishop

Sister Corita Kent (1918-1986) Immaculate Heart College & High School (1916-1981). Both high school and college were forerunners academically.

In the 1960S the sisters were proposing changes in how they prayed, worked, dressed, and governed themselves and they were in compliance with orders from Second Vatican Council and the Pope. However, Cardinal McIntyre opposed and ordered the removal of all Immaculate Heart Sisters, teachers, in his diocesan; his ultimatum was either conform to his wishes or seek dispensation from vows. Ninety percent (315 of the 380) choose to dispense. The prestigious high school and college closed. After Sister Corita discarded her nun's dress she located to Greenwich Village and Boston and continued to have a large following for her Art Work. The Smithsonian Institute has copies of her serigraphs; she leaves a strong legacy of developing fine innovative art of her own making and that of her students.

The phenomenon of the Sixties included President Johnson's 1964 Civil Rights Act. Racism and the Vietnam War were big issues. The spirit of the times was individualism and there were many issues with the Catholic Church including its views on abortion and homosexuality. Some historians would say that Cardinal James Francis McIntyre had neither the disposition nor the experience to deal with the new breed, well educated, Sisters of Immaculate Heart. The different social issues of the times cut deep and were an attack on truth itself.

Sister Corita gained international fame for her vibrant serigraphs. She combined sacred and activist ideas with her silk screen for popular art and posters. She has been referred to as a joyful revolutionary. She designed the 1983 Love stamp, reportedly one of the best selling stamps in history. There are many quotations ascribed to her.

Love the moment, and the energy of that moment will spread beyond boundaries.

Creativity belongs to the artist in each of us. To create means to relate. The root meaning of the word ART is "to fit together," and we do this every day. Not all of us are painters but we are all artists. Each time we fit things together we are creating – whether it is to make a loaf of bread, a child, a day. A painting is a symbol for the universe. Inside it, each piece relates to the other. Each piece is only answerable to the rest of that little world. So, probably in the total universe, there is that kind of total harmony, but we get only little tastes of it. That's why people listen to music or look at paintings, to get in touch with the wholeness.

Bob Kennicott's painting. I titled it: The Pope as A Pot

*Painted with a wax medium; an assignment in exploring from the classes of Sister Corita
at Immaculate Heart College, Hollywood, 1957*

Twenty two Years with El Segundo

I had completed practice teaching in the spring of '58 at the Vine Street School in Hollywood. The following two years were spent at USC earning a Master's Degree and taking a variety of other classes, primarily, psychology. I considered myself fortunate when I went to work for the El Segundo Unified School District. All twenty two years in the classroom were in that town. The name, El Segundo, is Spanish for "the second." This was the second largest oil refinery in the Los Angeles area when it was named. The local citizens were rightfully proud of this well run city government and their schools, three elementary, one junior high and one high school.

In the late 1950S there were several newspaper editorials praising that school district. Their budget provide many extras that included swimming classes for all students at the town's large indoor plunge; there were many specialists, nurses, a part time psychologist, a reading specialist, music teachers, a large curriculum center with sundry teaching materials, school libraries with librarians. All sixth graders had a week of outdoor schooling in the mountains. Grade level field trips were provided on the school district's buses, and playground supervision was frequently provided by trained people. It was a wonderful environment to work in as the facilities were most convivial and in accord. There were families that chose to locate in that community due to the excellent academic reputation of the schools and because it was a secure community bordering Los Angeles' airport, the Pacific Ocean, the oil refineries, and the Sepulveda Highway.

I experienced two events in September 1960; my thirty-third birthday and I began my first year of teaching at Imperial Street School. I was assigned to teach a fourth grade class. There were two classrooms at each grade level; my cohort and I had twenty two pupils each. It is said that a teacher will always remember the students from their first year of teaching. Now, fifty years later, I can remember quite clearly my first experiences of being in charge. My principal was a dear soul who wanted to assure me of his support and told me to send any disruptive child to his office. As a first year teacher one needs such support from his superiors. There was one little boy with attention deficit who was frequently disruptive. Having sent little Jimmy to the office on two occasions one might assume that both Jimmy and I had learned our lessons. In a weak moment I had forgotten what I had learned and told Jimmy that he was disrupting all of us and he needed to go to the office. He was meandering to the office when my ambiguous reflection kicked in! Will I regret sending him to the office? That was a mistake! Did I really want to spend my entire break time in the principal's office listening to his unrestrained promenading, conjecturing on life? Like lightning I flung the door open and got a glimpse of Jimmy way down the corridor, still under my jurisdiction, and called, "Jimmy!, Jimmy!, Come back!"

As wonderful as that school district was, it disappointed some youngsters as did/ and do/ most public elementary schools throughout the country. Jimmy was a very bright child and had high hopes to learn to speak the French language. Foreign languages were not/are not/ part of the curriculum for youngsters his age. Hopefully changes will be made. One year while teaching at the Early Childhood level I arranged for a friend, a former high school French teacher, to volunteer. "Miss French" was there two mornings a week and was besieged with adulation and appreciation from little ones who soaked up learning French like sponges.

Reviewing all the class photographs brings back wonderful memories as I thoroughly enjoyed working with youngsters of all ages and knowing the camaraderie of fellow teachers. Many occurrences seem insignificant, yet they're woven into the tapestry of life. After four years at fourth grade I transferred schools where I taught fifth grade for two years, and two years at sixth. From there I taught an accelerated primary class and another year a small class of pupils with learning challenges. Such was my hands on experience for working with two fantastic teachers in conducting our school's Early Childhood Program. Working with children of an early age is something like seeing miracles unfolding. Working with skilled teachers and skilled aids, plus caring volunteers, created a haven for learning. We managed our own classroom environment and shared our ideas and expertise. I believe it was my own negative experiences when I was a child in all the grades that set me up to excel as an adult working with an early age group. Certainly, that was a factor for my being there and I loved it! That age group enabled me to sometimes zoom between reality and the world of make believe!

For several years my aide was Barbara Schuttie who became a dear friend. Our rapport began when I was her son's teacher. Barbara was the mother of five and had a state license to operate a day-care center. The classroom was spacious and provided sufficient room for five or six Learning Centers, Reading, Math, Science, Art and other centers as needed. A center would have various activities whereby a child might act alone or with classmates, or with supervision. Some centers had audio visual equipment. The activities assigned to the centers were constantly being upgraded for ongoing challenging. The one center that didn't require changing was the art center with two easels. That was a most loved activity and such an essential experience for young children! Each of our three first grade classrooms had about twenty two children.

A large area rug was positioned in front of the chalkboard where the children sat for lesson presentation in reading, math, story time, discussions, sharing and such. Here, pupils might be assigned a specific activity for their time at a learning center. One math center had large dominoes designed for spreading out on the floor. A loving grandmother/volunteer came twice weekly for playing floor dominoes and teaching addition. That certainly assisted learning addition! Many games required body movement which was healthy for their age.

Unfortunately I don't play a musical instrument but made good use of recorded music. Many pupils learned to recognize Beethoven and distinguish the difference between Mozart and Tchaikovsky. Not all days were structured the same and music was worked in for discussions as well as for listening appreciation. I am a firm believer that music and art are an important energy source for learning at this early age. I am adamantly opposite to school districts cutting these areas from their curriculum, especially at the primary level! Art/drawing/painting and music are major building blocks in early childhood learning. One year I organized an art show that began in the classroom and grew to a showing at our city hall downtown; from there it went traveling to a couple of other city halls with the name: "The Sandbox Art Show."

Having had my own reading challenges I took extra care when teaching reading comprehension with the varied classes that I taught. I believed that deciphering reading material must include an understanding that distinguishes between poetry and common prose, and that legend differs from folklore, and the big difference between mythology and history.

Throughout the years I had kept in touch with some former pupils or their families. During my early years in the classroom the district had a policy for teachers to make two math groupings within the classroom; one group that met the standard math requirements and another group that was considered accelerated. There was a boy who didn't qualify for the gifted math group according to the testing requirement, yet he wanted so much to be a part of that gifted group. I had no issues with including him and with some additional help he did perform well. Years later I heard from him and he was jubilantly happy as he had become a math teacher. Among the former pupils that I heard from were those who became teachers. For some years I exchanged Christmas cards and received announcements of marriages and births of babies.

I thoroughly enjoyed my years of teaching. The experience of witnessing academic growth in students is likened to a spiritual path. I believe I received phenomenal blessings for twenty two years! To be prepared, dedicated and at the helm is an adventure with great satisfaction known to those teachers who have been there.

June 6, 1982, I was one of eleven being recognized and honored at our Retirement Banquet at the Crystal Ballroom, Hacienda Hotel, in El Segundo. The following is an excerpt from that program.

GERALD HEINTZBERGER

22 Years of Service to the District

Born: September 10, 1927

Grew Up: Mishawaka (Mis a wa ke)
Northern Indiana

Schooling: 1948 - Jepson's Art Institute, Los Angeles
1950 - 1954 Storekeeper, U.S. Navy
1958 - B.A. Los Angeles State College
1960 - M.A. USC - plus graduate studies

Jerry joined the El Segundo School District in September, 1960, starting out with a fourth grade assignment at Imperial Street Elementary School. (Jerry says that he is the last teacher from Imperial that year who is still in the District!) In 1964, Jerry transferred to Richmond Street Elementary School where he was to remain for the next 18 years serving two years each at 5th grade and 6th grade and then in the primary level in 1st and 2nd grades. He also taught accelerated and opportunity classes as well.

Throughout his tenure in the District, Jerry served on many District Committees. He was the P.T.A. Historian at both Imperial and Richmond Schools. He also served as Social Chairman at both schools (except that at Imperial the title was Sunshine Chairman!). As a member of the El Segundo Education Association, Jerry served as a site representative at both Imperial and Richmond Schools.

Jerry has been very happy working with Santo Prete and the staff and the current administration. He is especially grateful to his dear friend, Mrs. Watkins, and his aide, Mrs. Cummings, for all the help they have given.

Jerry has thoroughly enjoyed his teaching career in the City of El Segundo. As he stated, "El Segundo has been a big and happy part of my life and the memories will be recalled with fondness".

Jerry has no immediate plans for the near future. He will "hang loose" for awhile. With his 'green thumb' he'll be spending a lot of time in his garden working with plants and masonry materials. He'll spend time doing creative writing, traveling and seeing friends. He will use the leisure time to delve into all types of reading materials, from "how to" books to the "Dialogues of Plato!" Political, religious, science and social issues are attracting his attention, as is an interest in the world of business. Jerry thinks that two or three of these issues might draw him into activities in which he, in his own way, may make a different type of contribution to society. "I feel", said Jerry, "that the experience of having worked with youngsters of varying ages will have an influential effect on me for the direction of my future endeavors".

We wish Jerry Godspeed in all that he does as he commences a "second career".

1961
4th Graders
A Christmas Play

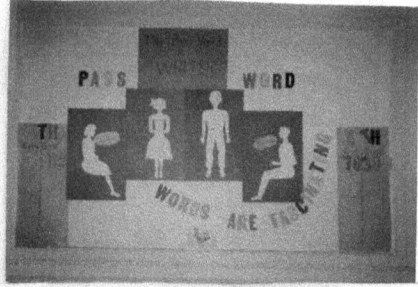

5th Graders 1965
A Game-
Pass Word

I don't suffer from insanity
I enjoy every minute of it.

2 nd Graders
Creative Writers
Experts

The Wonderland of Stories

6th Graders @ Outdoor School
San Bernardino Mountains 1966

The best way to bring up children
is never to let them down.

53

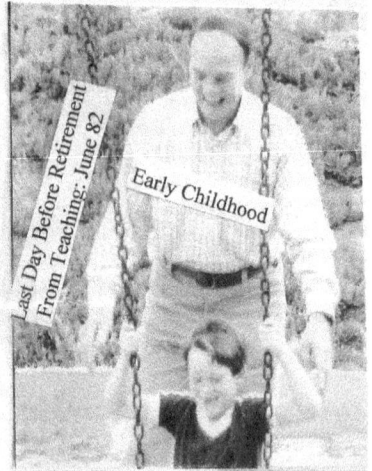

Last Day Before Retirement
From Teaching: June 82

Early Childhood

CLASSROOM

FOR EARLY CHILDHOOD

There are two ways to live your life. One is as though nothing is a miracle. The other is as though everything is a miracle. Albert Einstein.

A Tacher's constant job is to take a roomful of live wires and see to it that they're grounded.

Great men are they who see that spiritual is stronger than any material force, that thoughts rule the world. Emerson

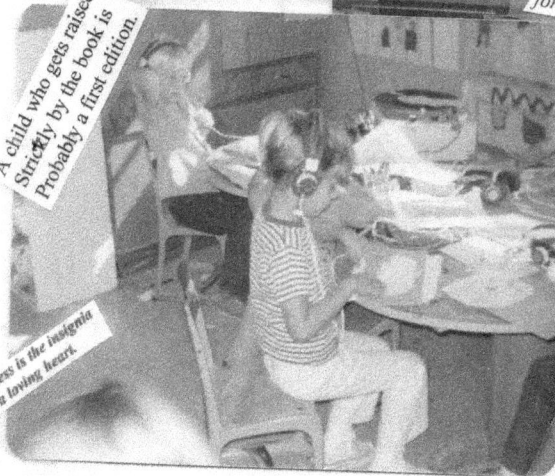

A child who gets raised Strictly by the book is Probably a first edition.

Kindness is the insignia of a loving heart.

54

WHAT FIRST GRADE IS ALL ABOUT

Who made first grade such good fun?
Made us feel like the extra special one?
Who filled our days with far away places?
Special friends and knowledge of wide open spaces?
Who do we wish could teach us our life through?
If you don't know by now, Mr. Heintzberger, it's you!

This little message is our way to say
Thanks for those special things you brought our way
Thanks for the tasks, they were such fun
And for the counting strips from 2,000 to 1
The time tests you gave us were so super and neat
The gold and silver stars we won were such a treat

What amazing worlds you opened to literature and art
Learning new ideas; and stars on the poem chart
Respect for our flag and for ourselves
The SCAPPER club was really unique
Rounding us and encouraging us to speak

We could sing your praises all the day
But there are some special thank-yous to say:

Thanks for teaching us to respect one another,
Caring for each person as a brother
You taught us rules are important, rules are a must,
But most of all you've taught us to trust
That teachers are caring and can be fun, too
We hope all our teachers will turn out like you.

The fact that you're leaving makes us sad
That other kids won't learn from you is too bad
You see, Mr. Heintzberger without a doubt
You are what First Grade is all about!

Jerry, Chuck, Herm, Bill, Kate, Berta, Henry - Collectively they produce 21 children

The seven siblings in 1967

Mom 1965
75 Y.O.

Mom at 55

Apartment Living – Meeting Fred

Summer of 1960 was the beginning of a new agenda for me. By September I was teaching and earning a steady salary. I was adapting to living in my own apartment and I was able to have kin folks stay as guests. My social circle of peers would likely grow. I was free to explore the Gay scene although I had no desire to be on the town. I did do some Gay bar hopping but felt that it wasn't for me. Dr. Bob and I didn't venture into the Gay scene as we were so preoccupied with projects at home. Gay bars were sometimes raided and it would be a humiliating experience, say nothing of a police record and losing one's career. Meeting like minded friends could be difficult as Gay socializing was suppressed in the 1960s. Brilliant minded Gays with job security clearances could easily became paranoid, and many did become so.

Mom arrived in California for Thanksgiving turkey as the snow blanketed Northern Indiana. It is gripping to realize how we view our parents at different stages of our maturity. A friend invited us to join him down the Coast to the Del Mar Race Track. That was a new and amiable experience for Mom and she had fun putting a few dollars on a horse that she got a "hot tip" on. My quiet demure little mother was just as intense when that race began as were those seasoned gamblers. Her flow of adrenalin reached a high as she was seen and heard hooting for her horse to win. I've known Mom to enter the spirit of the moment but this was more joie de vivre than I anticipated!

I saw Bob, Kay and Mike and Bill as I had an apartment nearby. It was a Sunday afternoon when I met a new friend. I was going to a coffee shop on the Redondo Beach Pier when I met Fred. We were each parking our cars when we exchanged a few glances and then a few words and we ended up sitting together drinking coffee. We established a good rapport by talking current events and card games. Later that week we met at a restaurant for dinner and two days later we met in his apartment for playing cards and a romantic encounter. Fred was an engineer, intellectually engaging, with a reserved demeanor, and three years older than I. We became mates for more than sixteen years. Our circle of friends was small and we both kept a low profile.

Fred was a regular for dinner and cards; his parents were included when visiting. Our parents enjoyed each other's company and we all played pinochle after dinner. Either Mom prepared dinner or we brought it home from the deli. Fred's mother enjoyed telling Mom about her work with her church's altar guild. His parents were devoted Lutherans and Fred was christened as such. Fred and I spent some weekends in the pleasant home of his congenial parents.

Sunday church service for me had been exploring some of the Protestant churches. A typical Sunday during Mom's wintering was to combine going to a Catholic church with an outing to explore developing areas. During the sixties California was realizing phenomenal growth and it was an adventure to see new communities springing up. There was a Sunday when I wasn't sure if the church steeple I saw in the distance was Catholic or not. When I expressed concern, Mom said, "Let's go there, we're all praying to the same God." That comment told me that Mom wasn't stuck in a time zone of the past. So many are.

I'm so grateful for having had my Mother spend those winter months with me at that stage of my life. Such extended stays were not only happy for Mom, but they were good for me as well. Leaving home at a young age when the hormones are so compelling must be a difficult period for any parent. I believe that's a reality of life. Spending quality time together after a degree of maturity has taken place was a real blessing for me as I was a normal nineteen year old Gay man seeking identity. I greatly appreciated that Mom was never judgmental about my life style and graciously accepted and enjoyed my friends. In 1967 when I received word of Mom's transition, I was scheduled to chaperone my sixth graders to the San Bernardino Mountains for a week of outdoor schooling. Instead, I went to the classroom and wrote a message on the chalkboard explaining to the class why a substitute would have to replace me.

My single status, never having been married was no concern to Herman even though he was happily married. In 1963 he and wife Betty and two young daughters spent their vacation with me. My Redondo Beach apartment was one block from the ocean and it was just natural that we should party during their entire visit. We packed picnic baskets daily and trotted to the sand where we dined alfresco with the thrashing surf beckoning us. The likes of such partying was reminiscent of high school summers in the mid 1940S when Betty and her girl friends rented a cottage for a week at Eagle Lake in southern Michigan. Of course Herman was invited and I could show up too. And, show up I did with buddies who drove cars. There are many small lakes in that region, and some, like Eagle Lake, had beer halls with jukeboxes. We took turns feeding nickels into the box and we danced, danced, danced! In those days a few hours of entertainment with munchies and cold drinks might cost all of a dollar or two.

Berta, Mom, Bill and Mike at my beach apartment

Mike & Bill entertain in their home: Mom, Jerry, Berta, Dr. Bob, Mike, and Kay Campbell

Entrance to courtyard

Manhattan Beach

In the summer of 1967 I purchased 2210 Pacific Avenue in the tree section of Manhattan Beach for $27,500. I was forty years old buying my first house. This would be my home for the next fifteen years. The house was twenty seven years old but neglected. The corner lot was 50 x 150 and the challenges to be creative inside and outside were there. I had a contractor for all indoor construction, including rearrangement of walls. I had the front entrance enclosed and my fun was in the designing and building patios and walls for the front, side and rear entrances, and sprinkle gardens all about. Those fifteen years were exceptionally happy as working with youngsters was fulfilling, and I had time for entertaining friends and relatives. In those days my idea for good recreation was a visit to the quarry for building materials and to the nursery for plants.

The happy day when escrow closed

For several years Berta was visiting regularly as husband Bill was consumed in his surgical work at the hospital caring for coal miners and fulfilling his boyhood dreams as mayor to bring his home town, Pikeville, Kentucky, into the twenty first century. This was the mid 1960S and her visits with me were thoroughly enjoyed. As an avid reader she had mail-ordered books and read feverishly the Harvard classics as well as a catalog of books on world

Berta approving my landscaping, having created a front courtyard

religions. She exchanged visits with family in Mishawaka but never visited our brother Henry in Philadelphia. Her visits to Manhattan Beach were eventful because she had an enthusiastic rapport with my friends. She enjoyed visiting my classroom and browsing in bookstores either alone or with me.

Berta's daughter, Barbara, came to the West Coast after graduating from Georgetown to work for some politician's campaign, and while staying with me had a clandestine rendezvous with her fiancée when I was in absentia. There were a number of relatives that visited in that small and charming Manhattan Beach house. Berta's daughter Mary and husband spent a day visiting while honeymooning in California. It was two year old Mary that I cared for back in 1945-46. In her adult years Mary and husband became prominent researchers in microbiology at Duke University. Mary died in 2008 at age 64 of cancer. Berta died in 1976 and is remembered in Pikeville with the Child Care Center named after her.

Henry and Vicky were staying in Pasadena when they rang the door bell on a Saturday afternoon. They were down from San Francisco and most distraught as daughter Emily from San Anselmo was hospitalized in Pasadena for her third or fourth brain tumor operation. I believe that was in 1979 when Emily was 33 years old. I had them moved to my home for several nights. When Emily was discharged from the hospital she spent the night at my place before they all flew north. That was when I met Emily for the first time. Her head was bandaged; she was weak and spoke softly. A few years later we spent time together and bonded.

Creating: The rear garden, looking down; my love to design and build

Mandy: When I was living in Manhattan Beach I was going to Inglewood, a distance of six or seven miles, a couple times a week to visit and look after my friend, Madolyn, more often called Mandy. Mandy was my neighbor when I lived at Dr. Bob's. From 1955 through 1960, Mandy and I developed a congenial friendship after many confabulating sessions over the side yard fence. A reprieve from studies in the late afternoons took me into the garden and there might be Mandy keeping an eye on her two Boston terriers, Timmy and Davy, while they did their duty. In time Mandy and I started looking after one another as well as those terriers.

Mandy lived alone and in 1954 while in her lower hillside garden, seventy or eighty feet from the house, she had fallen and broke a hip. She crawled on her hands and knees to her kitchen phone; after a few phone calls she disappeared to the hospital for a long stay. Our friendship developed after she returned home. When she decided to relocate to a condominium I became her trusted friend.

Mandy was born and grew up in Arkansas, a water colorist at an early age, in her declining years her interests were current events and working word puzzles. She had an unassuming demeanor with a dry sense of humor and no one would have guessed that during the war years she worked locally for the country as a spy. Mandy had appointed me as her guardian. For a time I was working with youngsters during the day and the evenings were spent with aging Mandy. During her last year I arranged for a full time live-in. At her death she left me a modest inheritance that I added to my account and watched it compound. I had already invested in what I assumed would be my retirement home, a duplex in La Jolla that I kept rented. That was when housing was affordable, so, when making out a new will in 1996, I decided to establish an endowment fund. At my demise the modest sum from Mandy, plus my contributions with compounding interest, will go to "The Gerald Heintzberger Early Childhood Fund," at a foundation in San Diego.

Among the possessions that I treasure most are gifts from friends who are now deceased. Several years before her death, Mandy wanted me to have a Christmas tree that was purchased the year I was born, 1927. It stands five feet high and is secured to a painted white box ten by ten inches. The limbs fold up onto the main trunk for storage. After the holidays it is wrapped with a bed sheet and awaits for the following season. I do believe it is a rare species of a tree as it is constructed of dyed chicken feathers and it is a convincing rendition of pine needles. In its entire eighty some years it is still a beautiful tree although a tad shop worn having decorations put on and taken off all these years.

Fred: Those fifteen years in Manhattan Beach were eventful years with teaching, seeing friends and having relatives as house guests. Fred and I spent much of our free time together. We complemented each other's reserved demeanor. There were nightly dinners together, card games, especially two handed pinochle, several camping trips to Yosemite National Park, seeing our small circle of friends, and of course, my many masonry projects. When Douglas Air Craft relocated to Orange County, forty some miles away, Fred purchased a house in that area. Our social lives changed to rotating weekends in each other's homes.

Fred was forced into early retirement in his mid-fifties. It was 1976. His distinguished seventeen year career in the second echelon of the space program as system design manager with Douglas Aircraft, with presidential citations, came to an abrupt end. He was involved in an entrapment. What happened: It was mid afternoon when Fred took a leave from work to keep a medical appointment. He was on his way when he stopped at a rest-room to relieve himself. It was there that he encountered a vice operation, was arrested and hauled off to jail.

In those days there were provoked and non-provoked raids by vice officers. After the arrest he was informed had he contacted his employer immediately, the arresting procedure would have stopped. Fred was so stunned that he went through the entire police nightmare and then went to work the following day. It was then and there that he was terminated. No one could have felt more heartache and despair and been more humiliated and depressed than he!

He was literally destroyed! The entire scene was beyond Fred's recall! Fred was in his early fifties and never sought employment after that! He had a modest savings that he drew on for living expenses. His pride wouldn't let him acknowledge what happened; he told people that he retired due to health challenges. He sold his home and went to live with his aging parents, miles away. He died at age seventy. I don't believe Fred's story, his entrapment, has ever been told to anyone until now.

Fred's termination affected me immensely! I realized what happened to him could happen to any innocent person who might have appeared problematic. Fred was so protective regarding his security clearance that he wouldn't step foot in a gay bar, and to be arrested! Rigidly, circumspect and upright Fred, with years of dedicated patriotism, allegiance, classified military security clearance, arrested! Unbelievable! For a time, my zeal for patriotism flattened as the so called perils of society sunk in!

Morality of the Era

What was it like to be arrested on a sex charge in the 70's? During those years there was a social stigma associated with all sex outside the marriage contract. Homosexuality was outlawed and designated as a disgraceful sin. An unmarried middle aged male suspected of sexual misconduct and arrested was presumed guilty by many regardless of his innocence. For someone like Fred to have fought the arrest and appear in court, with or without newspaper publicity, would have been more traumatic than the silence he chose. To have hired a lawyer and to have gone to court would have promoted tremendous anxiety for Fred and his family. Walking away and announcing that he was retiring due to health created closure from the legalities of the courts.

Recognition of homosexuality was against the law for many years leading to the mid 20th century. To speak out for homosexuality could put one in jail. In 1951, Edward Sagarin (1913-1986) with pseudonym Donald Webster Coy, a prominent writer of sociology, wrote that the fear of homophobia, the fear of sexuality, was society's challenge. He wrote: "There is no homosexual problem except that created by heterosexual society." He argued that homosexuality should not be discussed as a moral or social issue, but as a human rights issue. The challenge shaped a profusion of writing that flourished. Before a healthy acceptance of Gays were accepted in literature, such writers presented unflattering stereotypes. Interest with varying degrees of understanding homosexuality grew. Even the vocabulary changed: homosexuals prefer the term Gay

In 1951, Harry Hay organized the Mattachine Society which would become the father for many organizations that were devoted to outlawing entrapment and the oppression of Gays. While Hay's interests may have furthered the Gay movement, it may also have reversed the course for a time as Hays was a committed Communist and expressed many radical ideas. Nevertheless, Hay's impact was strong. In 2010, there was a three month production off Broadway chronicling the creation of the Mattachine Society called, The Tempermentals.

During the mid 1950's the hunt for Gays and the hunt for Communist in the United States were prevalent; those times could be merciless. Hollywood legends who were mistakenly identified as Communist were literally destroyed as was the actor John Garfield. Those police raids for Communist declined with a demoralizing recourse, but the hunt for Gays continued. Fred's entrapment in 1976,was seven years after the Stonewall riots, as there were corrupt political pockets in cities known to be unyielding to organizations defending Gays, the likes of the American Civil Liberties Union (ACLU) and such groups.

Corruption in various forms is prevalent in all countries regardless of government. Corruption of Gays in the United States, where we pledge "liberty and justice for all," was, and is, a force to be dealt with. Fred's arrest was during the same decade that the National Lambda Organization was founded, (1971-73).

Without the likes of the Lambda Legal Association, present day Gays would still be living with persecution in a society of unchanging laws, policies and ideas. It is my belief that man's inhumanity to man is character assassination which I believe was the case with Fred's arrest, and many cases that the National Lambda Organization defends.

For some time the joyous get-togethers that Fred and I knew turned into solemn hours, heavier than time spent after the death of a loved one. Fred apologized repeatedly for being "a heavy" and expressed gratitude for the support I gave him. I believe it took months before the reality of what happened to him became a reality. His only vague recollection of that entrapment was walking into that place to urinate. He could not recall having been there at another time; he could not recall phoning his doctor to cancel his appointment; he could not recall what was said before being told that he was being arrested.

The months following required a grievous adjustment! What to do with his life? For sometime he divided his days between being with his parents and with me. Just being together was good; we attended to some masonry projects and played some board and card games, but our lives would never be as they were. Considering the various contingencies, Fred could not bring himself to accept my idea that he could make his home with me. At the end of two years he had sold his newly acquired Orange County home and went to live with his aging parents some hundred miles from my home. The three of them maintained a close relationship as they were involved with church activities.

Fred's arrest haunted me then and continues to sadden me to this day. When I reflect on his arrest and the lives that it changed, it seems unimaginable. By my account this was an "Arrest by Problematic Circumstances."

****

The hallmark of courage in our age of conformity is the capacity to stand on one's convictions ---- not obstinately or defiantly (those are gestures of defensiveness, not courage) nor as a gesture of retaliation, but simply because these are what one believes. Rollo May

San Diego

I had spent twenty two years in the classroom. With Fred's move I wanted a life change. It was June 1982, three months before my fifty fifth birthday when I retired from the work that I loved! I had accumulated many treasured memories working with pupils and fellow teachers. Good teaching at any level is nurturing the soul and the mind. By contrast, I believed I could better improve my retirement income by buying and improving property than had I stayed in the classroom for an additional ten years, until age sixty five.

For years I kept tabs on the inflated prices of real estate and fancied that I could estimate current prices. I had fun winning wagers from friends by predicting what houses would sell for. Eight years previous, in 1974, I purchased what would be my retirement home that I kept rented. My next home would be near downtown San Diego on a canyon rim overlooking Mission Valley. I enjoyed the challenge of landscaping and doing my own masonry projects. I hired a kitchen design center to create a state of the art kitchen to enhance the investment.

With this move to San Diego I had a field of exploring to do. A short distance from my home was Tijuana, Mexico, just an hour's drive and I was in its adjacent country side. There were sights difficult to relate to. There were lean-to sheds perched into the muddy hilly terrain, most without basic amenities that housed families! The contrast was less than ten or fifteen minutes from my home to downtown San Diego with a diversification of inviting attractions. Balboa Park with many nurturing museums was a magnet for me during the total 14 years I lived in the greater San Diego area. For a time I volunteered as a docent in San Diego's first public school. Opened in 1865, the one room Mason Street School was located in the Presidio of today's Old Town, a desolate area back then without greenery. This was the time when I stopped smoking cigarettes and decided to remain square from marijuana and all drugs. I had tickets to just about every live theater production in the city. The outdoor theater in Balboa Park had grand stage productions as did The Old Globe Theater with a diversity of theatrics. Coronado had its own attractions including a small diner theater that I frequented. There was so much to learn, to see and do!

I had three different residences while living in San Diego and enjoyed entertaining in all. Emily's cancer appeared to be on the mend and she visited with husband and two youngsters and spent the night. Henry and Vicky were vacationing with two grandchildren and came for supper. For nostalgia's sake, I prepared an appetizer of "Mom's wash day soup." It derived its name because it was an expedient meal to prepare after a busy work day. The preparation required canned tomatoes, seasoning, spaghetti-pasta, and small scrumptious meat balls! Sourdough garlic bread topped it off! Fantastic! And they loved it! Sister Kate visited for a week. She was en route home to Indiana having vacationed in Australia. She shared many of her recent experiences but I didn't share all of mine. Today I would share more of myself with family as society has become more informed about my Ten Percent. I never acknowledged my sexual orientation to any family member. Yet, I spoke more freely about my friends with some members than I did with others. Perhaps they all knew I was Gay and respected my privacy by not broaching the subject of my not following the norm of being married.

After a time when the house and yard were ship-shape, I sold this "Grand Canyon Home" and took my earnings to the bank so it could work for me at compounding the interest. I had a good circle of friends so didn't relocate too far away.

Kate and Jerry overlooking Mission Valley in rear garden, Lomitas home

Shades of my eclectic art collection

Rancho Bernardo

Another investment was in San Diego's suburb, Rancho Bernardo. The area was developed in the forties around a golf course and the Rancho Bernardo Inn. For a time the community was viewed by some as being too antiseptic, too new, too many old people. The Inn had a traditional ambience of solemn elegance.

My work was readily visible for a major undertaking. I designed and had contractors construct an enclosed courtyard for the front yard, and used the same manufactured cement building blocks to enclose the entire yard. There was a huge neglected pine tree with needles that "liked to needle" the swimming pool and that was taken out. Five men worked with superhuman tactics to engineer that tree's removal. The enclosed area didn't allow for a vehicle to enter and apply chains around the massive root to pull and do the drudgery. The roots must have measured a minimum five feet in diameter and must have weighed over four hundred pounds. Two young men hoisted that tangled root system on their backs and carried it to their truck in the street.

In time the yard and house were transposed to a haven of privacy for kindred living. The surrounding terrain consisted of gentle flowing hills with streets that surged with the curvature of the land.

When that enterprise was completed I rewarded myself with a week's vacation to Santa Fe, New Mexico. I joined a small group of sixteen or seventeen sponsored by two college professors; she had her doctorate degree in music, his doctorate in art. They were an attractive middle aged married couple, she a former nun and principal of an elementary school. They acquired a following for their local tours as well as tours to several European countries. This tour was orchestrated around the Santa Fe opera season where performances were in their outdoor theater under the stars. Opera lovers couldn't want anything more magical. Brenda was methodical when planning any tour and explored it alone or with husband before taking guests. Visitations to museums and historical sites along route were carefully planned including menus and drinks at selected restaurants.

High-octane happiness is a blend of gratitude, service, friendship & contentment.

Faith that stands on authority is not faith. The reliance on authority measures a decline of religion.   Ralph Waldo Emerson

Trudy and Jerry pool side. As Walt Whitman said: "Every cubic inch of space is a miracle."

Living well and beautifully and justly are all one thing. Socrates 470? 399BC

We must make choices that enable us to fulfill the deepest capacities of our real selves.   Thomas Merton

The curious paradox is that when I accept myself just as I am, then I can change. Carl Rogers

Compassion is not just a religion or spiritual subject, nor a matter of ideology, it is a necessity. Dalai Lama

I thank God for my handicaps for through them I have found myself, my work, and my God. Helen Keller

Example is not the main thing in influencing others. It is the only thing.   Albert Schwertzer

Maybe in time evolution will produce men too civilized to quarrel about it.

Switzerland & Holland

That vacation was the beginning of new expectations in my life creating a propensity for travel. For the holiday season of 1989, I visited niece Barbara and husband Willis in Geneva, Switzerland, and cousin Jerry Meurs and wife Trudy in Utrecht, Holland. With such gracious hospitality I wondered why I waited so long in accepting their invitations!

Barbara managed "The Body Shop" boutiques in French-speaking Switzerland while their two daughters, Ashley and Grey, were in school. Will's work schedule with World Health was arduous but we still found time for several luncheons in time honored chivalrous inns where fireplaces were aglow as snow adorned the countryside

Barb took time off and the five of us visited ski resorts and historic sites. The Chateau de Chillion visit located on the shore of Lake Geneva was reminiscence of life in former centuries. I value the hikes amid the snow in Old Town Geneva. A white Christmas was reminiscent of growing up in Indiana and ice skating on the park's ponds. Here in Old Town Geneva, in 1989, is where I experienced my first roasted chestnuts from an elderly park vender. I was having a story book experience of savoring roasted chestnuts betwixt flickering snowflakes.

The frosty winter air stirred me physically and mentally. Coming from sunny California and bundling up in winter gear was fun. Old Town Geneva became a favorite destination for historic remembrances. There were larger than life statues of Martin Luther (1483-1546) and John Calvin, men of the 1520 Reformation. Geneva became an intellectual center for the Protestant Movement. It was Luther's thesis concerning indulgences that directed activities toward his reforms, as well as social protests against the Church and the Nobles for holding all the wealth.

My education of such Church history was limited. The nun teachers I had in grade school had merciless feelings for Luther, the heretic. I can attest that travel, like reading, broadens one's perspective. History of the Renaissance, 14th through 16th centuries, the transition from medieval to modern times reflects evolution; and now, it is our time, today's fleeting time!

An evening that was thoroughly Swiss Culture was when we attended a Christmas program by Grey's complying fourth graders at her public school where French was spoken. It was a delightful presentation! Our Christmas Eve was at home for opening presents with Will capturing the spirited occasion on his recorder for the children's grandparents in New York State.

This perfect vacation had to end. Getting better acquainted with Barbara and Will and getting to know Ashley and Grey was delightful. Listening to Ashley and her dad playing carols at the piano poured out holiday merriment.

When I left for Holland I hadn't completed my project of securing all the asbestos tiles to the ceiling of their basement rumpus room. Of course I can fault my hosts for my unfinished project as they prepared a full agenda. I knew I wanted to return, and return I did, on several occasions!

Cousin Jerry and Trudy were at the Utrecht train station to welcome me in the late afternoon. I left Geneva with overcast weather and there was rain during most of the ten or twelve hour trip. The following morning we went to a huge outdoor flower mart where Trudy bought plants to take home. They lived in a two story row house that had a den they used for a nursery as they loved caring for plants. I thought it incredible to have such a vast flower mart in the dead of winter in an open air mart! The Dutch have some exotic customs, but wonderful!

A night at Rummy Tile with great competitors, Cousin Jerry and wife Trudy

Both Jerry and Trudy were retired so we traveled to different cities where I met cousins for the first time. I had no connection in Arnhem with my mother's family, but did with my father's family. A trip to Doesburg where Pop grew up was a top priority. I met many cousins and all spoke English as that is part of the school's curriculum. Cousin Jerry and other cousins were retired from merchandising, several cousins were jewelers, a couple in civil services, and all were gracious to me. However, the candy factory was no longer there. Being a bachelor, and probably a Gay man, was of no concern. Holland has been free from Gay discrimination for years.

Amsterdam with several historic art museums was a priority. We saw Rembrandt's, The Night Watch which was indeed awesome if in size only. It is curious that so many early paintings by Dutch artist used dark oils. Cousin Jerry said that weeks pass when the sun doesn't shine. People have been known to experience depression due to the constant over cast. Perhaps that explains the desire for plants in their homes and the dark oils used by the Dutch Masters.

It was a disappointment that the Van Gogh Museum was closed during my visit. Nevertheless, when I returned home I began painting for the first time in many years. I had accomplished a few painting techniques and used a lot of bright colors right from the paint tube. My paintings weren't Van Goghs, but they weren't dark like the Dutch Masters.

There was another Amsterdam visit that wasn't to be found anywhere near home. Cousin Jerry and I strolled about in the red light district. Shopping was made easy for those on the hunt as the women of the night displayed themselves in the windows of their unit. These were row houses and it would appear that those who could afford the bay window setting charged more than those with a single glass window. That's just my guess.

Researching my Dutch roots with Cousin Meurs

A night on the town with Will, Barbara, Ashley & Grey, Geneva, Switzerland

It's in the Genes

One evening Jerry and Trudy invited our cousin Tom Wamelink and wife Erika to dinner. Tom and I would be meeting for the first time. When they arrived Cousin Jerry met them at the front door, out of sight from where I was seated. When I heard the exchange of voices I was taken aback with the husky gravelly voice of this cousin Tom, as it was identical to our deceased Uncle Bill's voice. I knew this Uncle Bill, but Tom didn't. Uncle Bill and my father were brothers and they were brothers to Tom's mother. When Tom stepped into the living room I was even more dumbfounded with his facial features and his body structure with weight distribution. This cousin Tom might very well be Uncle Bill in all respects! I became speechless as I looked at this cousin! Every gesture was exactly that of Uncle Bill's. As he sat in the chair he leaned slightly forward with his right arm flung across his right knee, his left elbow bent bringing that hand to rest on his thigh. This realization left me dumb founded! If gene pools could only talk!

Barbara had an experience during her college years that left her astonished. A girl friend had complimented her on several occasions saying how pretty she was and that she was reminded of a friend that she knew back home. Her

Photo circa 1915 is of Grandfather's Candy Factory Store in Doesberg, Holland

observations must have been uniquely defined as they were repeated several times and always had a note of mystification; "It's your facial bone structure, it's your mouth, it's the same beauty quality." The friend's last observation was: "Yea, you and Moira...you and Moira Heintzberger have that same beauty quality." At that moment Barb realized that she was being compared to her cousin. Barb's mother and Moira's father were brother and sister. The friend had no way of knowing that they were cousins. Barb had never met Moira as distances were great.

Empty pitchers full of memories.   Barbara, The home inspector - La Jolla

La Jolly Sunroom - a magical addition   *Musician Will at home in Geneva*

Expanding Spirituality

Relocating to San Diego in the early 1980S brought about changes. I became a regular member at Unity Church in Vista, a nearby suburb. I found Unity and the Church of Religious Science similar devotionally. Ernest Holmes, founder of the Church of Religious Science, sponsored a radio program. A repeated theme was, "Getting on Center." That phrase has been used by religions to mean to center the heart, mind and feelings. It encourages peacefulness, love, confidence, creativity and harmony. I also found by reading Deepak Chopra's philosophy that there is inspiration in his writing of ancient wisdom and today's science.

Sometime back, Mom sent me Emmet Fox's (1886-1951) book, *The Sermon on the Mount*. Fox was a New Thought Spiritual Leader from the Divine Science Branch of New Thought. I identified with him and a pattern of reading followed that included most of Bishop John Shelly Sponge's contemporary works. As an Episcopalian Bishop, his books include, *Why Christianity Must Change or Die, Living in Sin,* and *Rescuing the Bible from Fundamentalism.* These books are favorites because they revitalize my thinking for the "Spiritual/Humanist" that I was converting to.

Acquiring the audio tapes of anthropologist Joseph Campbell was a source of great validation to my own beliefs. His writings, *Inward Journey, The Myths and Masks of God, The Hero with a Thousand Faces,* are fascinating stories. Some of his folklore reminded me of images that danced around in my head, my attentive deficit head, during my formative years. He captured the spirit of primitive societies by acknowledging their every moment was spiritual, the oneness of everything. Their's were living mythologies by accepting the mystery of all creation, rather than a made up mythology to support man's churches.

Campbell was brought up Roman Catholic, advanced beyond, and became an eminent scholar, a foremost interpreter of myth, from stories throughout the ages. He believed that intuition is a faculty that will advance the human race. He died at age 83, in 1987. He believed that the human species is evolving and is on a path to discover a mighty multicultural future. His admonition was: "Follow your bliss. Find where it is and don't be afraid to follow it!"

As the white candle in a holy place, so is the beauty of an aged face.
Joseph Campbell

Leasing Property

The time had come to move to my La Jolla "retirement headquarters." I decided to rent the Rancho Bernardo house. I had dealt with renters and always had pleasant experiences. That was not to be the case with this new middle-aged couple. After they had been in the house a year they claimed that the house was infected with mold that made them ill to the point that they couldn't hold a job and had mounting medical bills.

One of their tactics was to wear me down so that I'd walk away from the house and deed it over to them. They moved a house trailer onto the driveway and decorated the house's exterior with bright red streamers and a number of large signs declaring that the house was "Contaminated." They demanded money from me as the air quality made them too ill and they were financially broke. My insurance people were involved in a process that lasted several months. This case was in part responsible for establishing new insurance laws regarding "mold" as this was a copy-cat maneuver. These people were con-artists who had a past and present history of suing. They came from New Jersey where they had a trail of law suits. Here they were suing a hospital and the doctor of her mother at the same time they were suing me. While I lost rental income and paid them to get out, they vanished after they failed to appear for the lawyer's deposition. I was exasperated, having had the integrity of my investment undermined, but was rescued by a real estate broker who was interested in purchasing the house for himself. He had enough experience with similar outlaws that he dismissed the seriousness of the situation.

An infrequent acrylic, 1990, The Magician's Chair

Welcome to La Jolla – Meeting Keith

Ultimately I took residence at what was going to be my long term retirement home in La Jolla. All my brothers visited. Chuck and Dorothy drove out from Indiana to visit here as well as when I lived in Rancho Bernardo. Bill and Nell visited with daughter Joanne, and Herman, like niece Barbara, was a regular. Henry and Vicky visited one afternoon and Chuck's son visited twice.

The building, a duplex, consisted of two townhouses, a front and a rear unit, each had two stories. The location was just a few blocks from the Pacific and walking distance to the village center. My enthusiasm to upgrade any building that I lived in always won out and renovation on both units soon began. I had owned this real estate and kept it rented for over eleven years. I contracted to have the rear unit, the owner's unit, walled in with six foot fencing made of red wood lattice painted white. That fencing was secured on top of a three foot high planter that had a depth

of three feet making a nine foot wall. That planter was home to a bountiful assortment of plants from native to exotic. I had contracted the Four Season Builders to construct a large solarium that served as an all purpose room. In the evening it became a dining room with the fragrance of fresh flowers and several hundred tiny white lights strung throughout the plants. All windows and doors in both units were upgraded to stylish French. It was indeed an exciting place, encapsulated in a secret garden!

One day I stopped for lunch at the Gay Caliph Restaurant Bar in the Hillcrest area where bartender Margaret would be serving her specialty lunch. It was there that I met Keith and we became partners and did extensive traveling for several years. He was Mr. Conventionality. His resume read like creative writing. Keith was former president of his town's town council as well as president of his social service organization, a retired banker, a board member of the local symphony, a former FBI man, a war hero who, with some crew members, survived their plane crash in Philippine waters and witnessed other crew perish in a fiery explosion. Keith was a widower with adult children and referred to himself as a "Jack Mormon" because he enjoyed social drinking and an occasional cigarette. For several years we shared living in each other's Shangri-la's. He was three years my senior. Keith owned five time shares and claimed that they were good investments only because they made sure they were used. And used them we did!

My travel diaries are full of impressions of foreign destinations that make travel so exciting and educational and occasionally what is alarming. When I was 64, in 1991, Keith and I took a five week trip to Europe. The Los Angeles airport had me go through the sensory testing several times. In doing so, my money belt with passport and wallet was left behind. I was seated aboard the plane when I made the discovery! To all horrors I was able to retrieve it just seconds before takeoff! In Geneva, Barb and Will hosted us before we left for a one week in London where Keith did a home exchange, and two weeks in Germany and Austria where we stayed in time shares.

Another year Keith had exchanged his Hawaiian time share with Barb and Will for their home. During that visit we explored Switzerland and drives into Italy. We traveled with local currency from adjacent countries, plus, our credit cards. When driving into Italy we didn't anticipate so many tunnels with costly toll fees. On one such trip we encountered three tunnels and had used all of our currency. Two of our three credit cards were not acceptable and the one that was had just expired two days earlier! I don't recall how we got out of that crisis, but I do remember a line of cars behind us waiting for us to move on.

We no sooner unpacked when we were packing for the next trip. We took a number of trips to Europe. Another long sojourn was to Australia and New Zealand. Snorkeling in the Great Barrier Reef was certainly an "eye illumination," a delightful wonderment! Bill's daughter, Moira, was living in Armidale, centered about 300 hundred miles from Sidney and about 300 miles from Brisbane. While Keith and I were staying in Brisbane, Moira and her two teen-aged sons drove down to met us. Moira was a shining example of a good diplomat for her adopted country and introduced us to a traditional Aussie cuisine: "You can't come here and not have chicken pie," she admonished. On their return drive to Armidale they phoned that their trip went smoothly. It took six hours for the 300 mile trip and at no time did another auto pass them, so isolated one can be in that country.

For several years Keith and I were world travelers. Some trips were to time share resorts, a couple with elder hostel, there were six or seven ocean cruises. My favorite city was Christ Church in New Zealand. We were there for only a day but I felt an abundance of energy in the air. That was the one place I wanted to return to but didn't. I collect "milk pitchers" as mementos from countries where I've traveled and use them at home to decorate. They all shine with happy memories, especially New Zealand.

When traveling in Europe our transportation was either by car rental or a Railroad pass purchased here in the States. The itinerary for one of our rail tours began in Madrid, Spain where we stayed several days just to visit their museums. The Prado Art Museum was a daytime adventure while late night dinning was joining the native population in merriment street cafes. In Cordoba we visited a Catholic Church that was enclosed by a huge Mosque. In Seville we encountered a gang of seven or eight Gypsy children that ran up and formed a chain around us. What could be taken for a friendly welcome was an intent to paw for money. We pushed them off by throwing our arms in the air and yelling! Our time share in Marscille was a tenth floor condo overlooking the Mediterranean Sea. It was

there that we lunched with friend and former La Jolla shop owner who took residence in Spain because she couldn't afford her medical expenses in the in the U.S. As our train passed Monte Carlo I was looking forward to going home.

In October of '92, we flew to New York to board a train for Montreal where we'd attend an Elder Hostel at the YMCA. After a socially delightful week at the Hostel and enjoying the beauty of that all encompassing city, and visiting Quebec, our itinerary was to train to our home towns, Mishawaka and Milwaukee. October is a magical time of year in New York, Pennsylvania, Ohio and Indiana, with all the foliage in prairies and cornfields turning to an assembly of wondrous colors in the crisp autumn air. I had been back to my childhood stomping grounds several times, but on this occasion, viewing the country side from a train coach, gave rise to pounder bygone times. I found myself reflecting on my forty five years since I left permanently. I had no regrets for having left and wondered what my life would have been like had I stayed. Would I have encountered angels or demons considering my Gay Gene and the history of changing times?

As the train pulled into the familiar railroad station in Mishawaka, Lo and behold, there was a greeting committee with Herman heading them up with his boom box booming! Such fan fair! It was truly a surprise home-coming! Kate, Herm, Chuck,

I'm at Hoover Damn with the perfect tour guide!

Dorothy and some of their kids, Nancy and Ross, and Kathy drove all the way from Athens, Ohio. Even the aroma of the home town air had a nostalgic taste! The trip was enlivening and we were treated regally. Keith was so taken with my kin folks in Mishawaka, real "Genuine Hoosiers!"

Another royal visit was in Las Vegas where we visited Brother Bill and wife, Nell. Keith was so impressed with the tour of the Hoover Dam that Bill gave us. Bill's knowledge of that dam's history, the various components that were required, the endless finite details; Bill had all the facts in order. Several times Keith exclaimed that Bill would be a grand ambassador for the U.S.

In March 1993, we flew to Washington D.C. and were greeted by a snow blizzard that altered our plans. The eighteen days included a timeshare in Fredericksburg, Virginia, where we visited Civil War Sites. Both Keith and I had relatives en route. Niece Mary for whom I cared in her early years was living in Durham, North Carolina. She and husband were associated with Duke University Medical Research. That was a full day of visiting and taking photos. In Fort Walton Beach we visited a nephew doctor that I remember as a two year old bouncing on all the furniture including the piano keys in that old rented house in Chicago with raw silk curtains. In Clearwater I met cousin Rita for the first time. She was the daughter of Uncle Carl, the uncle who had demons that Pop tried to help. Rita came to this county as a war bride from Holland. It was a busy week in Key West as some college students took over the resort.

Nice, France, will be remembered as the city that showed remarkable concern to their tourist! On a balmy Sunday afternoon in a neighborhood park we were surrounded with high spirited people congregated to hear a band concert. Keith needed to rush off to the lavatory. When the band began playing, I heard my name being called out above the orchestrated music. It was Keith! He had stumbled and fallen on the poorly patched cement walk! He was being guided and held up by two strangers while blood dripped from a deep cut on his forehead. The kindly strangers walked us to the nearby first-aid station which was a police station. From there we were taken by ambulance to the hospital some distance away, with the sirens screaming! The cut required professional stitches. The ordeal took from three to four hours. A surprising factor of this episode was the minimal cost, something around twenty or thirty dollars for everything; the ambulance, the emergency room, the professional attention, stitches, tetanus shot, the complete caring. For a week Keith pulled his hat down covering as much of his black eyes and patched up face, but that made him appear more like a hoodlum than ever. Vanity be gone!

Keith & Life's Complexity: Keith and I complemented each other in numerous ways. We had similar interests in reading material, music, travel; our temperament was alike as we were both outgoing, even our spirituality was similar although we were swayed by different forces. He was raised Mormon and as an adult identified as such. I was raised Roman Catholic and as an adult identify as a Spiritualist/Humanist. When not traveling together we

Snorkeling at the Great Barrier Reef

were together in one of our homes, three miles apart. I can't say how Keith might fault me in some way, but my concern with him changed from feeling beguiled to making a prediction. Keith could be charming under the slightest provocation but he had a hang-up of being seen in public with a male companion and was immediately compelled to explain himself to strangers. It may be on a conveyor belt in a department store in Sidney, or on a mountain hike with Yodelers in Austria, I knew that a testimony was forthcoming. He was so self-conscious of his sexuality, being viewed with a male friend that there was the inevitable announcement: "I'm a widower."

Real difficulties can be overcome, it is only the imaginary

ones that are unconquerable . Theodore N. Vail

Emily (1946- 1990)

I started living in my "retirement" home around 1984. A short time after settling I began hosting Emily, the niece I had met several years previously in Manhattan Beach and who visited me with children when I first located to San Diego. Emily's health challenges grew more severe and she wanted to pursue medical treatment at the Livingston Wheeler Cancer Clinic in San Diego. A major part of their treatment was having many glasses of carrot juice and colonic cleansing. The clinic attracted patients from all over the globe as it was considered the possible last hope.

Emily and I related well. We both enjoyed board games and sharing values. We bonded and I was a good sounding board for her woes. She was a child of The Sixties, sometimes a rebel with a cause.

Emily was happiest in Birkenstock sandals and a simple frock. She enjoyed journalism and attended to an array of writing. Her work studio in her San Anselmo home had several old fashioned printing presses that were her pride and joy. Emily received favorable reviews from her limited editions of old European folk lore. When rewriting such stories she changed the male hero to a heroine. In addition to configuring the story, she made woodblock illustrations, selected choice paper, set the type, printed the story and hand bound each book that contained fifteen to twenty five pages. Each book was signed and sold only to a few select collectors.

Emily was the mother of two adolescents at the time of her visits; her husband was an engineer employed in the oil industry and a skilled creative craftsman. Emily and Peter were emotionally involved in restoring their home in a historic neighborhood when her father gave her some unwanted advice. The home reconstruction required some periods of unsettlement while living in the house. "Can you imagine my father criticizing us for having our children in a house that he believed was disorderly? You owe it to your children not to expose them to such living conditions!"

As a child Emily disliked being reminded of her father's academic achievements. At a young age she felt that her parents were "more into each other than their children." Emily cited an occasion when her mother was feeling low and

111

wondered aloud if seeing a psychiatrist would help; her dad said nonsense, there's nothing wrong.

Emily shared a story she had written about her seventh grade experience. She was extremely distraught with a nun's discipline and complained to her parents about the distress and sorrow she was experiencing. Her father gave her the same advice that her great, great, great, grandfather told his son: "Don't complain to me about it or I'll have to discipline you, too." So much for the tradition of passing on family values! Emily wondered if the stress of that unhappy year planted the seeds that caused the stress that caused the brain tumors that caused ongoing operations!

Emily died at age 44 having made medical history. For several years while convalescing at home in San Anselmo she was seen traversing on her three wheel bicycle going about her business. Emily made numerous friends as she was active and loved by many, especially the San Anselmo arts and crafts groups. There was a huge gathering in attendance for her funeral.

Emily a sharp contender at our card and board games. Here we are in La Jolla

Sometime around 2002, I had a visit from Emily's daughter, Victoria and husband. The topic of Emily's lifelong diaries was brought up. Victoria said that her grandmother perused some of the diaries and exclaimed: "I didn't know how unhappy Emily was back in those days."

Henry & Vicky

Henry and Vicky were dating at DePauw University in Greencastle, Indiana, in the mid 1930s, the depression era. Vicky's parents were immigrants from Poland. When she started first grade she spoke only Polish. As an adult she was bilingual and had a charming speech pattern. Many of her expressions were emitted with a breathless ebullience that engulfed her personality. I thought she exuded an aura of sexuality the likes of Zsa Zsa Gabor. Unlike most women who would dress down for an evening with their husbands, Vicky would "doll up" for her man. During a visit to my home she made the declaration that: "Every man should have his own Marilyn Monroe." The comment was made with a thrust that inferred, "See what you're missing by not being married!"

I do believe that in 1937, when I was ten, Vicky and I had bonded. There were several Sundays afternoons when Henry took me with him when he visited Vicky in her parent's home in South Bend, some twenty miles from our home. While I grew up not knowing any cousins, Vicky had many and they all knew how to party and enjoy themselves. Their back yard was converted to a festival of jubilance! The piano was wheeled from the living room into the rear yard where Vicky's sister took charge. Vicky and her brother played their accordions and Papa Szaulewicz, a former musician in the Russian Army, danced the exciting hopak folk dance with knees bent and buttocks just inches from the floor while the feet went flying back and forth! Exciting! Such was tradition. Tables were stretched together to accommodate an assortment of delicacies. Days of preparation must have gone on as there was such an abundance of meats, salads, veggies and scrumptious desserts! Such was their Polish culture of merriment. It is appropriate to cite here that during those days of the Great Depression, cities like South Bend that had a concentration of any large new foreign group, had tensions, particularly racial tension. Vicky encountered a degree of prejudice in her childhood at some of the schools she attended.

Henry began his career as an actuary on the East Coast and retired on the West Coast as president of the company, a subsidiary to the Eastern Firm. They were living in a San Francisco suburb home when I visited them. My visit preceded Emily's illness that brought them to Manhattan Beach. I flew up early one Sunday morning and returned that evening. It was apparent that they chose not to have accommodations for overnight guests. I did meet two of their three sons. One spent the afternoon in the kitchen with his fiancée, and the other son and wife joined us for supper in the sun room, picnic style.

Of my four sisters-in-law, I discerned that Vicky's perplexities gave cause for concern. There were times when she and I shared a warm hearted identity. At age sixteen I was the best man at her wedding to Henry in 1943. However, with the passage of time our relationship became strained, thwarted. Over the years it appeared that Vicky was cutting Henry off from all of his one time family, his siblings. Henry and our sister Alberta had an age difference of fourteen months; they shared a close togetherness not only in their formative years, but in their early adulthood in Chicago. Yet, during the years Berta visited me from her Kentucky home, she flew to San Francisco only once to visit her brother, and that lasted for a few hours before she returned to my home in Manhatten Beach. Over the years my phone calls to Henry were increasingly cut short as he'd say: "Got to go now, Vicky's calling." Additionally, his business connections took him into my residential area, but he never phoned or visited. It was natural for me to wonder: "Were his suspicions of me as a Gay man his reason to maintain an estranged connection, or was it Vicky's influence? Her control?" In 1950, Dr. Bob sent photographs of me in navy uniform to my siblings. All responded with a note of thanks except Vicky and Henry.

For many years Henry and Vicky received recognition and honors as Organizers of Friends of The Library in their Bay Area community. Their volunteering was celebrated as they maximized a most generous income for their library. Thus, they were pillars of their community. Henry's other interests were playing bridge and golfing, genealogy research with apparent countless hours of endeavor, and for a time he painted beautifully in a precise manner.

There was much about my brother Henry that I admired, but I do believe he was an "enabler." I find it provocative to ponder his persuasions. From my perspective he enabled his wife to sway his thinking, and she controlled him with her admiration of him. It wasn't until I started writing this autobiography that I learned of their falling out with one of their three sons, some thirty five years past. Could it be his badge of honor, his allegiance to some learned principles that were formulated and fostered in those early years at Saint Joe that directed him to be thus ---- Swayed? Conditioned? Trained?

We usually see things not as they are, but as we are.
It's sad that our ancestors did not live long enough to realize how smart we are.

Anyone who has written an autobiography learns he can make two kinds of enemies with such a book. The people you mention and the people you don't.

Henry, 12/25/1915 - 5/27/2004

I was residing at the Springs address when Henry's son, Victor, phoned to tell me that Henry had a heart attack and died on the eleventh green while playing golf at his country club. That evening Vicky phoned and invited me to the pending memorial service. The service was held at their Country Club and an Episcopal priest presided as their Catholic parish priest wasn't available. I did not attend for sundry reasons. The obituaries in the newspapers did not mention that Henry had any siblings.

As stated in the Introduction, I started writing memoirs after January 2008, after I read Henry's incomplete autobiography. I went in search for Henry's completed manuscript and located his name sake, Hank, on line. Our first encounter. Via e-mail and phone I learned that he had a falling out with his parents in his sophomore high school year. He deliberately flunked out because he loathed the course work, resented the harsh cocky Nazi like discipline thrust upon him by some of the religious teacher/brothers in the courses that his parents insisted he take. Later, when he announced that the girl he intended to marry didn't meet with his parent's approval, he lost their consideration, no longer was he regarded in the same manner as his older brother and his twin. Hank spoke about separations, the enduring scars that have cut into his life. Hank became a farrier, a blacksmith, a wrought iron artist, and relocated out of state where he and wife home schooled their two bright children who are now young adults, the pride and joy of their communities. Away from parents, young Hank wasn't told which political party to vote for and he was free to be his own person.

Henry and Vicky enjoyed vacationing frequently in Palm Springs. Our last visit together was after I moved to Palm Springs, a year before he died. Their 53 year old son and 21 year old grandson would join us when they would be passing through the area as they frequently did on business. This was Victor, the twin to farrier Hank. I had met Victor that Sunday afternoon in 1974, but don't recall any conversation with him. In that sense I'd be meeting him for the first time. I was sorely disappointed when Vicky refused my invitation for lunch in my home because, "Such an arrangement would undoubtedly interfere with the boys' golfing plans." The five of us met in a small family type restaurant near my home. As usual, Henry was most gracious, exhibiting a hearty convivial exterior. At the end of the hour and half luncheon, I asked Victor if I could ask him a question. He said fine and I asked, "What was the most important lesson you learned from your parents?" He thought for a moment and said: "Family values!"

In Defense of those Nuns and Henry

In defense of those nuns I surmise that they, like all of us, are part of this world's evolutionary process. In my lifetime there have been monumental changes in all phases of life, and especially with the Catholic Church! The beginning of the 20th century was aligned with a poor economy and the church was a place for young adults to turn to who had a need to leave their childhood home. Religious Orders lured numerous youngsters into their way of life with a promise of an education and assurance of security and a ticket away from home. In some cases immature youth were forced from home with no other place to go. Early in the century my Uncle John found passage from Holland to the U.S. by joining, in Holland, the Holy Cross Brothers at Notre Dame, Indiana. When his indenture was completed he married a girl from a Protestant family and converted to her church and made his livelihood with the U. S. Postal Services. Even today the Catholic Church educates young men from third world countries to minister here at home. Today, several Catholic schools in my home town have been consolidated and there are lay teachers. It is difficult to believe that the majority of nuns that I was assigned to were fulfilled with their life style. I believe that many worked at becoming something they were not and they became, "Righteous phonies."

I believe in an odd sort of way, Henry, too, was a victim of the treatment he received from those early nuns. As a child he would have fulfilled any woman's maternal fantasy as a very bright and obliging little boy. In a classroom of forty or fifty he would have been favored. (I have witnessed and felt such favoring.) I believe he developed a strong self righteous image, exemplified and nurtured by those nuns who doted on him, and they became a dominate part of who he was at an early age. He developed convictions, beliefs that he regarded as honorable pertaining to life's complexities, such as marriage, raising children, political affiliations, and life styles worthy of acceptance.

Vicky had encountered a degree of discrimination in the 1920s. Perhaps for that reason she developed a strong desired to keep her husband to herself. Individuals and ideas that didn't conform to her and Henry's needs/thinking were kept at a distance or were cut off; that can be called: "Family Values." Their capacity for accepting ideas or people outside the confines of their comfort zone was limited. Such can be the controlling power of religion! He was my brother and one can say that he and his wife belonged to the "Religious Right Group."

On the Move – Laguna Hills & Life in the Coachella Valley

My La Jolla sanctuary had a stairway that didn't take kindly to my ailing knees. It wasn't the stairway to heaven that I once hoped it would be. My aching joints told me to move to one story living quarters and sell my "retirement retreat." At this time Keith required assisted living and we saw little of each other. Leisure World in Laguna Hills, a few miles from Laguna Beach, held an allure for me with its geographic location between Los Angeles and San Diego. In '97 I sold my retirement retreat and bought a home in Leisure World, and thus a new division began. Remodeling was limited to putting in quality flooring, a new kitchen and a rose garden with assortment of heights and colors. In time, to my dismay, I realized that the dampness here was similar to that which I had moved away from in La Jolla.

In 1999, when I was 72 years old I had bilateral knee replacement at Saddleback Memorial Hospital in Laguna Hills. Prior to surgery, several people warned me not to have both knees replaced at the same time. I regret not heeding their advice as ordinary walking these past years has been stressful. The hamstrung muscles remain tight. Adequate exercise was, and is, arduous. My endurance level is low. It all adds up to gaining weight and developing a heart condition. Recuperating after knee surgery was painfully challenging! Getting to the mail box was a chore as it was in a cluster of boxes located some distance atop a steep incline. The homes on Sosiega West were designed to accommodate wheelchairs; after extensive correspondence, my efforts for a mail box were acknowledged by Senator Boxer, and the Post Office did install a box for easy access. The box was placed in front of my home the week I was moving out.

While on the mend I house sat a friend's home in Palm Springs. Again, my interest was seeking real estate. Much of Palm Springs is the reservation of the Cahuilla (ka-we-ah) Indians. The upthrust mountain range with Mount San Jacinto's 10,800 feet protects the valley from coastal dampness giving dynamic energy to the mountain range with its rocks. Areas in this valley are especially acknowledged and revered by the unspoiled natives as spiritual oases with mineral pools, hot springs and changing seasons. Many new arrivals like myself are pleased to discover a composure of spirit in this Coachella Valley. As my close friends have made their transitions, I find myself more alone with a blissful contentment to reflect and write my memoirs. In adolescence my ability to write was hindered, but that restraint found new direction here.

I did purchase a condo adjacent to Palm Springs, in Rancho Mirage, one of the Springs Country Club's 710 homes. Three years after knee surgery I was under the knife again. This time the knife was at the Eisenhower Hospital. The aortic valve was replaced with a pig's valve and there was a by-pass. One thing for certain is the fact that coumadin is a medication that's not for me! It is a rat poison! After heart surgery I spent several days in an outpatient facility before returning home. Mike came from San Pedro and insisted on spending a few days. Had he not been there, had I been alone, I would have bled to death the second night home. I was in bed when my nose began bleeding. I called to Mike and together we tried to stop the flow, but to no avail! While Mike insisted on calling 9-1-1. I was pleading not to as I didn't want to return to any hospital, even though blood was saturating my body and bedding. It was past midnight when I was back receiving a transfusion of several vials of blood!

That emergency trip required another three day hospitalization. The day I returned home I had a repeat performance of nose bleeding! Imagine that! Again, an ambulance late at night, no pleasure jaunt! However, this second time we were able to get to the emergency room without delay where they packed my nose and I was home in six or seven hours.

The last two houses I purchased were intended to be my permanent home, not an investment to fix up and sell. I would probably be living at the Springs address today if a leak in the roof and a broken water pipe under the foundation hadn't occurred almost simultaneously. In that time frame a real estate person appeared with clients who were interested in that Stephens Court address. That afternoon it was sold and I was released from the agitation of repair. The following day I made an offer on a nine year old house in Del Web's Sun City, in Palm Desert, ten miles further east. I was entranced with the healthy palms and citrus trees; one of Del Web's largest lots! In time I realized that I took on too much responsibility and expense with a miniature orchard, rock spa and water fall. Most importantly I realized that I relocated too far away from good friends. In the fall of '06 I purchased a condo in Palm Springs. Like millions of people, I was buying and selling at a poor time and took financial losses!

Perhaps it was the stress that I was experiencing at that Del Web location that brought about the feeling that my transition was near. I did have a defibrillator inserted in May 2007 to replace the pacemaker from September '06. Bill's grandson, James, from Australia and his delightful bride visited for a few days. I had met James twelve years earlier in Brisbane and regret that I wasn't my usual animated self during their visit. While James was reminiscing about his parents, memories of my mother came over me. After mom's funeral I was scanning her book by E. Stanley Jones, (1884-1973) a Methodist theologian, titled, Abundant Living, when a strange degree of immortality came over me. On the back page, in Mom's hand writing, the following: "Happy the man who bears within him a divinity, an ideal of beauty and obeys it, and an ideal of art, an ideal of science, an ideal of country, and the virtues of the Gospel." During Mom's twilight years, while wintering with me, she expressed herself on several occasions by saying: "Life is a wonderful grant! To have experienced the beauty of nature and all its wonders is truly a miraculous gift!"

During this time frame I sold three choice oil painting. I missed them sorely as they gave me much joy. Due to my low energy I discouraged niece Barb's visitations. She was making yearly visits from Europe, Thailand or Pakistan or wherever husband Willis was working with the U.N. After the Del Web property sold I regained energy! I settled in my present Palm Springs condo. Contrary to my better judgement I purchased a condo on Indian land where the buyer has monthly fees which are subject to increases. Not a prudent investment for me.

However, I am blessed to be enjoying the tranquility and beauty of my energized surroundings. As one approaches the front entrance, located on the side structure to this two bedroom, den, condo, one passes roses that I planted and care for. There are gardeners who attend to a profusions of colorful flowers facing the street. From the living room and kitchen one overlooks a sea of golf course green with several ponds where mallards visit and bathe. There are sand traps to challenge golfers, and palm trees of enormous height are framed by the mountain range. The palms and other trees are roots for a variety of birds from tiny colorful finches to the sassy croaking black birds or ravens. Beautiful white herons with their eloquent wing span and elongated legs make appearances as do a few migrating akin. The patio is a berth for potted plants, tomatoes and herbs, basil, oregano and thyme that I use for creative cooking. There is Charlie, nature's incredible humming bird that hovers in dance formation around my head between sips of nectar. Charlie can't possibly be more than a few ounces, yet, we share this mystifying manifestation of creation!

A highlight in 2008 was being asked to be the witness at a Gay wedding ceremony for two dear friends. In California, Gay Marriages were recognized from June through November. There was a small gathering in the sanctuary of the couples beautiful garden on the Sunday in October when they tied the knot that bound them legally, although they were already committed emotionally.

Constructing My Declarations

With advancing years and health challenges, I enjoy being in my own quarters. I enjoy listening to Mozart and I find some old show tunes scintillating. I do t r e a s u r e solitude and can be away from television and radio for several days. Silence is an invitation to meditation. I find the computer to be a marvel as I can travel anyplace at any time with the luxury of silence. Oh beautiful silence! It has so much to say! When I moved to the desert I attended sessions to volunteer at the hospital and the local museum. I didn't follow through due to lack of stamina. For a short time I volunteered at the Children's Museum.

Some current events have been of concern that I've written many letters to newspaper editors. In 2004 the presidential race was lost by the candidate who won the popular vote but lost the election due to the Electoral College vote of 271 to 270! At that time I wrote to over eighty newspapers declaring my protests to the wars in the Middle East where three major fundamental religions exist. I believe that the nature of war is: "War Begets War!" Political concerns must be settled in boardrooms, not blowing up countries! Bush's Iraq war which began in 2003 is said to have had 106,000 casualties of solders and civilians! With the proliferation of arsenal in this nuclear age, civilization can be quickly annihilated. I have faith and am optimistic that this 21st century will be more stabile and will avail wisdom in leadership that will shower a safer horizon.

In 1994, scientists claimed that there is a gain of 90 million people each year. In 2009, scientists state that an environmental problem is earth's over population. The U. S. Census Bureau estimates current population to be 6.773 billion. In 1994 it was estimated that by the year 2050, the population will be nine and a half billion! Present day food production and supply falls short for providing adequate food for today's people, how will people survive in years hence?

Societies are bound to change! The fabric of the times promotes many changes. Religion cannot be as unchanging as some theologians preach. Some do a disservice by clinging to outdated myths and legends. How can a society be moralistic and not be realistic? Many politicians show lack of concern with their idea for the sanctity of life by rejecting all abortion rights and assisted dying procedures. Those issues should not be judged by regimented religious beliefs of past generations that lead to broken lives. They are matters singly between man and his Creator. Shouldn't religion concern itself with over population and famine? There are throngs of worn out ailing bodies who have no desire to stay alive, yet they are consumers. I asked: Where did this society's morality come from? Jesus was circumspect and gave no such instruction. He took issue with the Pharisee's holy outward appearance that concealed hypocrisy.

Social Media changes society: In literature and art there is Dante's *Inferno*, the most celebrated writing of the 14th century, describing hideous demons with Satan, god of the Underworld masquerading as the Angel of Light. Such was the subject matter for the esteemed fine artist of the period. Large oil canvases of satanic force casting pitchforks at monstrous looking humans and beasts in hell's all consuming fire! Such master pieces of art were the religious subjects of the day breeding an array of people for institutionalized behavior. Today, they hang in museums for their artistic and historic value, and they can be given credit for demoralizing the human soul. Such is part of our Christian heritage.

The evolution of thought, of education and change, is a given, it is upon us! Presently, a small minority in society adheres to "Greed is good; money and power are king!" Conversely, in many parts of the world evolution is advancing with assistance from The Human and Civil Rights Movements. I wonder, perhaps "sense" is better stated, that there is some celestial energy directing many Gay people like myself to "come out," to claim our birth right. We are concerned with more issues than Gay Marriages, Women Priests, or Gays in the Military. Many of us have hope for the disadvantage at home and in third world countries, the homeless, the hungry, the unschooled, those in institutions. We Gays are creating a social catharsis! Unlike former times, talents of Gays with their contributions are being recognized and accredited. As issues with society's morality are being played out on the world stage, I believe men of greed will take heed and have a change. The lessons we all are learning are from one another. Every new born should have the birthright to fulfill his God given potential. No unwanted child should be forced onto this world with a population compounding among alarming afflictions. The judiciously Planned Parenthood Orders are vital steps forward for forming nourishing societies that could save today's civilization from a self destructive overly populated planet. My quiet Gay gene is striking out for preservation of humanity.

Fragile Planet Earth needs us! I deem that many of us Gays known to have had discrimination in generations past, can bring about a healthier climate for times to come. The concerned brotherhood of man faces challenges with that political minority who can, and will do, much to reduce global suffering. A healthier climate will develop when power driven egos have a change of perspective, a change of heart. That should include the Pope's power! Denouncing the use of condoms in third world countries, denouncing abortions for young girl rape victims! That is horrifying to me! Its unchristian and unconscionable! As we Gays claim our place at the table, we hear platitudes, clichés, from our opponents such as: "Family Values," "God is on their side," that they are allied with the Constitution and the Bill of Rights. The World's Civil and Human Rights Societies need be vigilant against such individuals and groups.

Issues! I Belong to that Ten Percent

Homophobia: It appears to me that during the past thirty-five years more has been written about homosexuality than during the entire twentieth century. In his 480 pages titled *Homophobia A History*, Byrne Fone's provocative writing chronicles the evolution of homophobia, the fear, the not knowing. The historian, Louis Crompton, in his book, *Homosexuality and Civilization*, (2003) records that most Christian and Jewish religious held irregular attitudes to such. On the battlefield with Alexander the Great, during and in the highest ranks of the Han dynasty in China, in the bisexual poetry of Arabs in Spain, and among the Samurai in Japan, same sex male love flourished.

Our Evolving Times: Man's sexuality is reflected in the times. I lived through the 1930s, 40s, 50s and 60s when attitudes toward sex appeared to be expressed differently with each decade of the twentieth century. There were locales that set their own parameters on sexual acceptability that led to corruption and persecution. The prudery from the Victorian Era left its mark. There were laws and imprisonment for defending homosexuality! Emancipation for Gays is involving decades of reform! The Mattachine Society (1951), the Lambda Legal Association and the American Civil Liberties Union, (ACLU), and others, all are enterprising benefactors seeking equality for today's Gays.

Homosexuals in the Military: In the 1920s and 30s homosexuality was dealt with as a criminal act, a move that saw a huge number of Gay Sailors and Soldiers imprisoned. Between 1941 and 1945 the armed forces used psychiatrists to determine sexual preference, and homosexuality was viewed as a mental illness. Persons who admitted to have engaged in homosexuality were unsuitable for military service. In 1943, regulations were declared banning homosexuals from all branches of the military. Fifty years later, in 1993, President Clinton introduced the policy of, "Don't Ask Don't Tell." In 2011, President Obama declared that homosexuals may serve in the military without discrimination.

The Neurosis: Making laws that put Gays as second class citizens has brought about many conflicting suppositions. I believe those who are responsible for making such laws have "the neurosis." In 1973 the American Psychiatric Association removed homosexual from its Psychiatric Manual as it did not meet the criteria to be considered a mental illness. Many bisexual males join the military to identify themselves as straight in compliance with social mores. I suspect that there are military divisions on bases that would shut down if all Gays and bisexuals were identified and discharged. The disparaging denouncement that government has perpetuated on Gays is an invitation, a validation, for bullying.

They Died for Our Freedom: In his 784 page book, *Conduct Unbecoming Gays and Lesbians in the Military*, 1993, Randy Shilts (1951-1994) brilliantly writes: *"In World War II, Gay soldiers died on the decks of the USS Arizona in Pearl Harbor and spilled their blood on the sands of innumerable South Pacific Islands. They died at Inchon and in the rice paddies of Vietnam. In more recent years, they parachuted into Grenada, suffocated in the rubble of Marine barracks in Beirut, and dug foxholes in the shifting sands of Saudi Arabia, Iraq, and Kuwait."*

Compassionate Coupling: Randy Shilts devotes pages describing incidences from 1778. The Continental Army was not without its homosexual heroes as were all wars in our country's history. There are documents that tell stories of the homosexual encounters during the Civil War. In his profusion of writings, Poet Walt Whitman records nights he slept with different soldiers while in Washington D.C., in 1862 and 1863. Whitman recognized that the forms of custom can smother the wish to love and be loved and bring peace to the world.

Catholic Dictates and Tensions: While the U.S. military dealt with homosexuality in the 1930s and 40s as a criminal act, the strong arm of the Vatican, Pope Pius XI, in 1930, declared birth control a Grievous Sin! God created sex for married couples to procreate! Women were to have babies as that was GOD'S Commandment! Catholics converted to Protestantism, others became agnostics. Religious tensions were evident in my home town regarding dictates from the Vatican. Today, years later, all age groups see common place advertisements for sex; erectile dysfunction, the likes of Viagra and Cialis are acknowledged as concerns for health and pleasure. Such sex acknowledgement in my youth was as unlikely as a weekend trip to Mars would be in this era.

The Phenomenal 1960s is noted for social changes with President Johnson's 1964 Civil Rights Act unfolding from a controlling climate. Riots were part of the total rebellion attacking social inequities. The Vietnam War was a big issue. The second Vatican Council was addressing changes. For Gays it was the Stonewall Revolt, June 27, '69. Six weeks later, The Woodstock Musical Festival, four to five hundred thousand Straights and Gays celebrating the Humanity of Life with three days of partying that ushered in a new era with less control.

The Stonewall Revolt: The revolt at New York's Gay bar made such a brazen impact that every year since then in large cities here and abroad, parades are held to celebrate Gay Emancipation. The message is universal. We are inclusive in all races, all religions, all stratum of society, doctors, teachers, engineers, all trades and professions. We have Gay and Straight relatives. We do not conform to a stereotype; our values differ as we do not share the same family values, nor political views nor the same kind of entertainment. The Stonewall riots are to millions of Gays what Rosa Parks did on that Alabama bus in 1955, the Civil Rights Movement. Today, in many metropolitan cities there are Gay Men's Choruses promoting goodwill recitals that are well attended.

The Reality of Sex and the Times: Following this period of revolt, approximately from 1965-75, my perception of those times was a downward trend for the religious clout. After the events of the sixties there was a marked difference in attitudes regarding sex and the topic was no longer as unapproachable nor as secretive as it had been. Now, in this twenty first century, society is recognizing that Gays constitute a large percentage of the world's population, probably ten percent. In today's world there is a more realistic understanding of homosexuality in man as a spiritual/physical being. The majority of the younger generation can deal with such reform. Closeted Gays are coming out of the closet and are changing their lifestyle of charades. Medical men have published books for straights and Gays showing numerous positions for making love. Such defiance, such insubordination to the Vatican's higher ups!

Gay Genes in the Desert: Palm Springs has a chapter of the National Gay Organization, The Prime Timers, at one time over a thousand members, presently, about eight hundred, all senior Gay men. They circulate a monthly bulletin announcing pending social gatherings. If a study were made showing the percentage of members that were once married and are now either divorced or are widowers, and compared those figures to those men who never married, my guess is that the findings might be as follows. They'd be equally divided between the divorced/widowers and the never married. The former married would have two divisions: those who believed they are capable of having a healthy long term relationship with either male or female, and those who believe that it was a tragic error for them to have followed the mores of society and messed up their life and the female partner's life. The never married group would say they only imagined a partner/ lover of the same sex.

Remove the Blindfolds: It is unfortunate that some heterosexuals perceive Gay relationships as being primarily sexual when that is only a small aspect of being homosexual. Sociologists might well agree that proportionally there are as many strong Gay relationships as there are strong heterosexual relationships. I introduced friends that were blissfully together for 48 years. People who wish to be educated about my one tenth of earth's population will find a warehouse of information, including Gay spirituality, on the internet, in libraries and bookstores. To the uninformed the revelation of many great humanitarian figures in history who took lovers of their own sex will be of interest. There have been past cultures where homosexuals have been acclaimed and venerated. I am aware of such a devoted relationship among two brilliant clergy who revere their being together as a spiritual gift, as do other same sex couples that I know.

In my eighty some years on this planet earth the population has increased three and a half times, from two billion in 1927 to seven billion today. Is it thinkable that the earth's evolutionary process might be promoting homosexuality as a measure to check population growth? Is it absurd to wonder if the planet, in its wonderment of nature, of evolution, has its own conditioning? The bias that same sex coupling was taboo, sinful, was in keeping with the times. Regardless what the objectives were, either expansion for religious growth or a country's need for strong male warriors, either gave reason to shun same sex coupling. Where in the New Testament is homosexuality condemned? Is there a higher ratio of Gays today, and if so, is that nature's way to curb earth's population?

The Catechism Omitted Much: Considering the ancient cultures of world history, two thousand years is not that long ago. Thus, the Catholic Church's ascendancy on the world scene is relatively new. In twenty centuries it has captured some of the Jewish and pagan pageantry of bygone eras. In its efforts to establish authority, by demanding adherence to its beliefs, it has lost credibility. Such accounts include the Christian Crusades, the torturous Inquisitions where thousands were slaughtered by the Pope's command, having Galileo recant his support of the Copernican theory, a history of atrocities, the burning innocents at the stake, the invention of purgatory, the Protestant Reformation, (Martin Luther 1483-1546) with the releasing of souls by prayer and for money, selling pardons, dispensations and indulgences. These were some of the laws and events.

Sexuality is a Big Part of Who We Are: As a child growing up I knew nothing of the Catholic Church's dark history, but I refuted inwardly and passionately to the tactic's and preaching that repelled me. As I grew from puberty into young adulthood I refused to be shackled with guilt and sin as the Church was proclaiming. It was not just the Catholic Church but many churches preached fire, hell and brimstone instead of Christianity's message of brotherly love.

In today's jurisdiction to command authority the Vatican wants to instruct everyone how they should express their love in the privacy of their bedrooms! Men, who apparently have not understood their own sexuality, assume the decree that they should dictate to others how to conduct their sex lives. Based on their premise of what constitutes sin, society's "holy men," with conflicting mores have created sand castles. Celibacy is the church's issue, it is not physically natural, not part of nature, not in accord for healthy Straights nor Gays.

The Horrors of the Righteous: Religions that hold that their fairy tale teaching be unquestioned will indoctrinate when possible as I experienced in the 1930s. Bible Proverb XX11, 6: "Train up a child in the way he should go and when he is old, he will not depart from it." Such indoctrinations have been for both, good and overly zealous promoters of evangelism. Some religious homophobes will use any means to accost their opponents, even false moral censorship.

Human nature has conditioned humans, especially insecure individuals, to respond to social changes in accordance with their anticipation from the way their social group, their peers, will react to a given situation. One can be induced to ideas of prejudice, homophobia, when surrounded with people who echo each other for the sake of belonging. What can be expected when there has been years of discrimination against Gays by our own government? The song from Rodgers and Hammerstein's musical, *South Pacific*, 1949, "You've got to be taught to hate and fear, its got to be drummed in your dear little ear, you've got to be taught before its too late, to hate all the people your relatives hate." Such profound truth! Morality exemplified!

Irony of Free Speech: Oddly enough, one's personal concerns, the degree of freedom that one now enjoys as an American, one's sacred beliefs, the partner/lover one wants to live with, will only continue if religious preaching is not allowed to integrate with political policies. If religion is permitted to be inserted into government as it is FREQUENTLY called upon, what is to prevent a religious group from stepping in and taking over? The tides of time will account for change affecting societies either negatively or positively.

Another Religion in Control of My Life: If I could grant my own legacy for my country, it would be that separation of church and state be treated as an absolute! Politicians who would inscribe their dictates of their organized religion are highjacking spiritual and social growth for millions. Today's churches have their own web sites telling people how they are obligated to vote.

One such church organization asks: "Have you had it with the ACLU aiding activists, teaching that two men living together are a family?" Such zealous hatred against Gays comes from narcissistic people who are convinced that God has ordained them to be care keepers of people's souls/lives. They excel at preaching fear. If you don't follow their rules, their judgment dooms you to hell. Do as they say and you'll be "saved". They have huge followings because they excel with shrewd authority: "No one dare question or challenge their command!" Such incisiveness is a factor responsible for suicides of many young Gays and the shattering of lives of families. Men who are truly holy men work at being spiritual and do not preach fear, hate and destruction.

The Prerogative to be Me: A quote from Herman Hesse, in 1946, "If you hate a person, you hate something in him that is part of yourself. What isn't part of ourselves doesn't disturb us." The hate that some attest to homosexuals is their own insecurity of morality in the frame work of our social structure. Gay giants in all occupational fields have contributed greatly to the comfort, security and beauty that we all enjoy. Life on planet earth is evolving and we all are interdependent. We all belong to the same consciousness that is connected to the mysteries of life, planted in the solar masses of endless space. How arrogant it is to assume that humans on this earth are the center of the universe and that everyone be converted to the one "and only" true religion!

The Wonders of the Incomprehensible: Many discussions regarding world affairs end with such conclusive statements as: "Religion is the culprit; Religion has brought on all the world wars and misery and suffering." Throughout my grade school years we youngsters at Saint Joe were taught that our religion was a sure ticket to heaven. We were encouraged to pray for the poor pagans who didn't know God; they aligned their worshiping, their thinking, to the sun or to some aspect of nature. As a spiritual seeker, I believe there is no more honest reverence to our Creator than being in awe of the wonders of nature! God is so incomprehensible we can only begin to glean the wonders of all life, human life, animals of the jungle, life of the sea and in the air, majestic trees from acorns, the metamorphosis of evolution! With such mystification, such wonders, I could never connect, reconcile, that God, the CREATOR of everything, had an only begotten son (?) and because God loves man so much he sent this son to earth to suffer miserably and die for man's sins! (?) To revere God through THIS Jesus, and to know THIS Jesus exclusively through THIS Christian mythology, along with its dark history, is acknowledging a power ploy. Like countless people everywhere, I revere Jesus' philanthropic works as he was a great humanist/mystic. For me, the Vatican's Catholicism is a religion of political power with processional splendor to control at any time and at all levels. Its history is of world banking with revenue in His name and farfetched dogma of pious fraud. The Vatican has been its own shield for centuries. Jesus' teachings, the Beatitudes, have been overshadowed by church authority in favor of political gain. Over the years the Church has taken on "Articles of Faith" that they proclaim were revealed by God and are mandatory to believe! Such articles are "concealed in mystery," and mystery is the antagonist of truth. I believe those mysteries are twisted ideas that are contrary to the early founders of the Christian religion. Dogmatic theology is disruptive to many. When some teachings are disregarded, I believe earth's evolution will advance more peacefully. Jesus never claimed divinity. Like millions, I believe it is more reverent to believe that Jesus was born a normal human who became "Lord." To those who censure me of not being a Christian, I challenge them of not being a real Christian for their beliefs which were drafted and embroidered long after Jesus' mission. I believe Jesus mastered inspiration and spiritual comprehension with collective knowledge from ancient religions. He changed the course of history through his mysticism, contemplative prayer, transcendence of God by deep meditation, spiritual study and good works. He preached with divine inspiration! He lived simply. Adoration was not what He sought. He died guilty of insurrection. His sage message was: LOVE; to live a life of continuous love!

Integrity: I find that being in awe of the Pope's spiritual splendor is being vulnerable. The history of the Catholic Church reads of world power struggle more than spiritual enlightenment. There were some years of decadence with increasing conflicts and schisms of sordid mayhem among its hierarchy of princes, some popes were sexually promiscuous while wielding power and control that were paramount. Today's Catholicism is diminishing in membership in the advanced cultural countries while expanding in third world countries. With a history of forging for worldwide power and present day scandals of pedophilia, with ongoing cover up from superiors, I find such moral hypocrisies discerning to believe that the history of the Vatican has housed the "Vicar for the Son of God" for two thousand years! The present day successor, adored in finery with ruby red shoes, travels in a transparent super structure on the chassis of a Mercedes-Benzas, as he blesses the throngs of people. Being "in awe" of such spectacular theatrics is a commentary about the Vatican's ability to reign among a huge trusting populous. I ask: "If Jesus were alive today would He be a Vatican Catholic?"

"Age of Enlightenment" The early 18th century is sometimes referenced as such due to a period of great change. Benjamen Franklin, Thomas Jefferson and Thomas Paine were among the founders of our constitution who were deist and humanist and active in the secretive Mason's rituals. In today's political world there are those who want to do a makeover of these men to complement their evangelical affiliations. In like manner, today's quarrels regarding Jesus' birth and ascension are wrangled from sacred held inerrant beliefs to Jesus' simple teachings directed toward manifestation of love and fairness.

In our Enlightened Society: I believe that decisions, regulating man's private and spiritual life, need to include numerous points of view, not evangelical rules taught with zeal of an arrogant pathology of knowing a comprehensive God. The desire to control other people does not make obsessions right; they have fixations inspired by their take on "What God wants!" The procedure following what God Wants is to act in honor of God, be it wars, claiming to be the one and only religion, indoctrination of the young, and judging and preaching who is and who isn't acceptable to our Creator.

Advancement in Religious Growth: The heartfelt experiences of my early happy home life while being rebellious at a Catholic elementary school may have quickened my spiritual insights during my eighty-some years. I believe the advancements in the sciences that we have been experiencing reflect growth on many fronts and can well be considered "Advancement in Religious Growth." The history of ancient religions show gods born of virgins and ascended, as some people believe was Jesus' destiny. Joseph Campbell's (Anthropologist 1904-1987) life"s work discloses mythologies that we find so engaging. Different religions chose to select and keep some teachings as truths and refute others as too supernatural. I see Christianity with an overwrought mythology that tangled up its history, too often missing the spirit of Jesus. Many of today's congregates are ignorant of, or oblivious to, the Church's spotty record, but nevertheless refer to themselves as: "We're the faithful!"

Inspired Mentors: Until most recent years, with the advent of the internet, written ideas for change could take generations before being learned. Ralph Waldo Emerson (1803-1882) set the background for the many religious reformers of the twentieth century. He wrote: "Be not the slave of your own past. Plunge into the sublime seas, dive deep and swim far, so you shall come back with self-respect, with new power, with an advanced experience that shall explain and overlook the old." Mahatma Gandhi (1869-1948) India's great

Hindu political and spiritual leader, Prophet of Nonviolence, told the world in mid twentieth century: "You must be the change you wish to see in the world." He also said, "I like your Christ, your Christians are so unlike your Christ!" And, "Violent means will give violent freedom." Abraham Lincoln (1809-1865) did not belong to any Christian Church but was known to be very spiritual.

Education or Indoctrination: It is often in accord with what "they" suppose the laws of nature to be, or the laws of God. I believe that political and religious ploys are constant. One third of the German army responsible for the extermination of six million (6,000,000) Jews were Catholics! Adolf Hitler, (1889-1945) who formed the Nazi Party, as recent as 1933, was a baptized Catholic. In our society today there are seekers for elected government positions who have limited knowledge for the job, but they seek votes by exalting their love for God, country and family, while declaring their opponents as evil! Charismatic personalities can influence people and fascist type governing can be created.

Human Nature's Basic Needs: I identify myself as a Spiritualist/Humanist. I have faith in my own intuition and the rationale that science attunes to, and take issue with the forced dictates from organized religions, the likes of those that attempted to indoctrinated me as a child. It behooves societies to learn from the unborn. UNICEF tells us that half of all children in the world are desperately poor; many die from starvation, go unschooled, live short lives in utter poverty. Again I ask, how can society be moralist and not be realistic to changes in birth control? There are those who are aligned with the Pope's dictates to contraception! The deist,Thomas Pain, (1737-1809) who believed in God, a framer of the constitution, a controversial writer who was widely read, referred to Christianity as "Unedifying to man and derogatory to the Almighty."

As a Spiritualist: The inexplicable structure of planet earth in this brilliantly orchestrated universe has illuminated, for me, who I am; I am my own oracle. I believe in a Divine Spirit intertwined in all creation! Perhaps the Lord's Prayer illustrates my identity: "Our Father Who art in heaven."

As a Humanist: I identify with the National Humanist Organization. I aspire to the greater good of humanity by upholding human reason, ethics and justice. The 1964 Civil Rights Act has had on going effects for a more humane society. There are numerous organizations working for the brotherhood of man. Present day volunteering is at every level: large and small groups, young and old are abounding worldwide in poor and rich countries.

Opposition: I believe that great strides for peace will be made this 21st Century. There are those who cannot agree as they believe there is a cultural decline, too much debasement from our entertainment media. The degrading stories with violence, many with an exchange of foul language are breeding a percentage of individuals void of rational thinking. Thus, today's previews with atrocities!

Evolution goes on: I believe my intuition is aligned with evolution for man's progress during this 21st century. I have faith that world leaders will possess the necessary wisdom to defend societies against politicians who use the religious card to thwart population control. There are researchers in many countries all working for humanity's innovations to promote planet earth's evolution: Earth's atmosphere, global warming; water for thrust and bathing; food production to prevent starvation; education to understand social functions and energy; medical updates and numerous basic concerns. I am optimistic that a more realistic enlightenment of man's spirituality and sexuality will be advanced as it relates to developing morality and forms of custom.

I Developed Enlightenment: Writing for me has brought together the impact that we Gays have on society. With the changing barometer of time, many of us Gays will be more resolute as we accept ourselves as we are amid our intuition. We are healers and doers! As I reflect on the religious authority of my past, and today's obstructions to spiritual enlightenment, I am grateful that I can acknowledge greater concerns. There are core values for human dignity sought by World Wide Humanitarians in the areas of Civil and Human Rights, a revolution in consciousness! Such is our growing faith that furthers our spiritual insights where we chose to ponder for ourselves, our own conscience, our own human and spiritual concerns. As humans derived from a Divine Source we all have our own Divine God. I believe technology's role is to create with our Creator. I believe a moral code is within us and will be fully realized when the basic need for nurturing the whole of earth's population is met.

My sharing, from whence I came, will ultimately conclude with my soul traveling to that unknown light as my body returns to the soil. The lessons learned are that today's beliefs, today's truths, can be tomorrows falsehoods, be they religion or science. It is my faith that future generations will build toward a time when celebrations will ring out for having a planet where people of differing races, religions, genders and cultures have come together on this peaceful earth. Thus, this has been my journey on our planet as it follows its tracking in the midst of millions of stars in the endless space of the cosmos.

I have faith that the ongoing studies of humans in our social structures will be an impetus for celebrations! Gaining insights into facts versus presumed beliefs add assurance to moving upward with enlightenment. Society's inclusion to uphold "my ten percent" is in sync, I believe, with evolution. The spirit of man moves forward! That having been stated:

The death of dogma is the birth of reality Immanuel Kant

My Disquiet Gene Sings Out!

The Human Race is Evolving!

Instinct the nose of the Mind. Madame De Girardin

Knowing others is wisdom. Knowing yourself is Enlightenment. Lao-Tzu

God is to me that creative Force behind and in the universe, who manifests Himself as energy, as life, as order, as beauty, as thought, as conscience, as love. Henry Coffin

It isn't easy for an idea to squeeze itself into the head that is filled with prejudice.

We are not permitted to choose the frame of our destiny, but what we put into it is ours. Dag Hammarskjöld

Faith in oneself is the best and safest course. Michelangelo

The deep emotional conviction of the presence of superior reasoning power which is revealed in the incomprehensible universe, forms my idea of God. Albert Einstein

There is no devil, but fear. Elbert Hubbard

My Disquiet Gene Sings OUT!

Progress is impossible without change, and those who cannot change their minds, cannot change anything. George B. Shaw

I would rather stand against the cannons of the wicked than against the prayers of the righteous. Thomas Lye

Faith is not something to grasp, it is a state to grow into. Mahatma Gandhi

"What do you think of God," the teacher asked. After a pause, the young pupil replied, "He's not a think, he's a feel." Paul Frost

The greatest of all crimes, at least that which is most destructive and consequently the most opposed to the design of nature, is war; but there never was an Aggressor who did not floss over his guilt with the pretext of Justice. Voltaire

It is necessary to the happiness of man that he be mentally faithful to himself. Thomas Paine

A comprehended God is no God at all. Gerhard Terteegen

When you have decided what you believe, what you feel must be done, have courage to stand alone and be counted. Eleanor Roosevelt

Peace has higher tests of manhood than battle ever knew. James Whitter

A consciousness of God releases the Greatest power of all, Science of Mind

The kingdom of God is within you. LK 17:21

This above all: To thine own self be true. William Shakespeare

The light of God
Surrounds me,
The love of God
Enfolds me,
The power of God
Protects me,
The Presence of God
Watches over me.
Wherever I am,
God is.
Prayer Card

There is but one ultimate Power, This power is to each one what he is to it. Ernest Holmes

You don't live in a world all your own. Your brothers are here too. Albert Schweitzer

My story tells why I refer to myself as a Spiritualist Humanist

133

Each generation reflects, to a lessor or a greater degree, the dynamics of their time in history.

In 1927 My Disquiet Gene and I were born.

1927 Charles Lindbergh the first to make transatlantic flight, none stop, alone.

1928 Alexander Fleming & two other scientist discover penicillin.

1929 October 24, the New York Stock Exchange crashes!

1930 Pope Pius XI declares birth control a grave sin.

1931 The Hoover Dam begins - Franklin D. Roosevelt- finished in 1936

1933 End 13 years of prohibition. Iceland first country to legalizes abortion.

1933 Roosevelt in office; U. S. goes off the gold standard.

1934 Adolf Hitler & Hermann Goering eliminated enemies to gain power.

1935 Social Security Act signed by Franklin D. Roosevelt.

1935 Germany's Huremberg Laws which rescinded civil rights for Jews.

1936 Jazz grew in the bordellos of New Orleans & Speakeasies of Prohibition.

1937 Hindenburg Zeppelin catastrophe - 97 passengers die in explosion of fire

1937 Darwin's book: Genetics & the Origin of the Species.

1938 The Physicists succeed - The discovery of nuclear fission.

1939 Europe at war. Hitler invades Poland begins World War Two.

1939 Marian Anderson turned down by DAR to perform at Lincoln Memorial.

1940 First radio broadcast of the Metropolitan Opera.

1940 The Battle of Dunkirk lasted ten days - British victory with heavy losses.

1941 Japan's surprise attack on Pearl Harbor-War: Roosevelt stayed 3rd term.

1942 Dawn of the Nuclear Age.(Gas cost 15 Cent a gal; Ration 3 gal a week)

1942 Battan Death March -Japanese command forced 76,000; 54,000 finished.

1942 Japanese American forcibly interned to detention camps in U.S.

1943 Oscar Hammerstein's Oklahoma on stage a big success.

1943 Scientist begin decoding genetics. Cells were some sort of molecules.

1944 Invasion at Normandy - 2,000 ships, 4,000 landing craft, 11,000 airplanes.

1944 Battle of the Bulge. Land battle, more than million fought, 19,000 killed.

1945 Japan U.S. war ends after atomic bombs hit Hiroshima & Nagasaki.

1945 "The Cold War" approximately from 1947 - 1953 - With USSR

1945+ Tribumals Nuremberg Est. 5,709,329 Jews murdered in Europe ***

1047 Hollywood's hunt for members of the Communist Party.

1947 Jackie Robinson, the first black baseball player integrated to white team.

1947 Physicist at Bell Laboratory invent the transistor.

1948 Alfred Kinsey's research published, Sexual Behavior of the Human Male.

1948 Mohatma Gandhi, 78. ascetic, called "The great soul," assassinated.
1949 George Orwell published Nineteen Eighty Four.
1949 Hank Williams, Country & Maria Callas, Opera, become stars.
1950 Pius XII (1939-58) invoked infallible, Assumption of Mary to heaven.
1950 The Korean War begins - ends 1953.
1950 William Faulkner receives Nobel Prize for Twenty Century novels.
1950 Charles Schulz's comic strip, "Peanuts" with Charlie Brown & Snoopy.
1952 Dwight Eisenhower, Army re Normandy invasion, 34th U.S. President.
1953 George Jorgensen becomes Christine Jorgensen.
1953 Playboy Magazine's first issue uses Marilyn Monroe on its cover.
1954 Jim Crow laws ruled that school desegregation be implemented.
1954 Senator Joseph Mc Carthy began a witch-hunt re Communism.
1955 Rosa Parks defies boycott in Montgomery, Alabama.
1956 Construction of a 40,000 mile interstate highway system began.
1957 Soviet Union launched Sputnik, first artificial satellite.
1958 Fidel Castro assumes total power in Cuba.
1959 Alaska becomes the 49th state, Hawaii becomes 50th state.
1960 The first oral Birth Control Pill created by endocrinologist.
1961 Rudolf Nureyer, Russian ballet dance defects U.S. & requires asylum.
1962 The Berlin Wall added on to encircle all of West Berlin.
1962 By years end, The Beatles were the most popular musicians in Britain.
1962 Cuban Missile Crisis - Soviet Union & U. S. - President Kennedy.
1963 President John Kennedy assassinated in Dallas.
1963 Martin Luther King's speech in Birmingham, Alabama, I Have a Dream.
1964 Civil Rights Act, President Johnson completing what others started.
1965 U.S. escalates Vietnam War - Vietnamese torpedo boats, U.S. retaliates.
1967 Two assassinations: Martin Luther King, 39; Robert Kennedy, 43.
1967 First heart transplant - Dr. Barnard - Cape Town, So. Africa.
1978 A counter culture, Hippie Generation, Haight Ashbury, San Francisco.
1969 Astronaut Neil Armstrong, b 1930, took first steps on the Moon, July 20.
1969 Gay Liberation comes of age - Stonewall Inn Bar, N.Y. June 27 Revolt
1971 United States severs ties to the gold standard, basic unit of currency.
1971 T V "All In the Family," begins, Archie Bunker, Edith, Gloria & Mike.
1972 United States withdraws from Vietnam. 1954-75 military conflict.
1974 Roe V. Wade - legalized abortion in first trimester.
1974 The Watergate Scandal - Richard Nixon resigns -Gerald Ford-president.
1974 Technology - the pocket calculator becomes of age.

1976 Lebanon Civil War Begins -Christians massacre Palestinians & Muslims.
1976 Man made gene - the basic unit of heredity - capable of working in a cell.
1977 Anita Bryant crusade against Gay Right Laws. She looses her status.
1978 Year of 3 Popes! Paul VI died, -John Paul died @ 34 days, - John Paul II
1979 Three Mile Island nuclear power station took ten yeas to decontaminate.
1980 Ronald Reagan becomes president: Charles & Diana married.
1981 Personal computers come of age, the electronic era with microchips.
1983 Nearly 1,600 cases of Aids has been reported world wide.
1983 Drugs, "crack" produces homeless people.
1984 Indira Gandhi, four times Prime Minister of India, assassinated.
1985 Mexico had two major earthquakes, more than 7,000 in City killed.
1986 Chernobyl Nuclear Plant, Soviet Union's Ukrainian plant full meltdown.
1987 Jim Baker & Tammy Faye resign Praise the Lord Ministry; $$$$$$$$.
1988 Iran-Iraq War ends after eight years and a million deaths.
1989 East & West Berlin are united after destruction of "The Berlin Wall."
1990 Dr Kevorkian - violated the Hippocratic Oath helping people die.
1992 Clinton 43 %, Incumbent Rep George Bush 38, & Ross Perot 19 percent.
1993 World Trade Center explosion - 4 New Jersey Muslims Fundamentalist.
1994 L.A. 57 killed in earthquake: L A's 4 seasons, quake, fire, flood & drought
1995 Whitehead Biomedical Research shows new research for Y chromosome
1996 Record blizzard shuts down Northeast - N.Y., Washington, Philadelphia.
1998 Nobel Prize in Physics - Three men - two Americans & one German.
1998 Northern Ireland: Hostilities between Catholics & Protestants mount.
2000 Vice President Al Gore wins popular vote but looses to George W Bush.
2000 Medical Science develop first draft of genome - DNA.
2001 September 11, terrorist attack U. S. World Trade Center & Pentagon.
2002 Belgium legally recognizes Same Sex Marriages.
2002 Defense Secretary Donald Rumsfeld shows Bush plans for striking Iraq.
2003 Scientist concerned that human activities are affecting Global Climate.
2004 Tsunamis in Sumatra Island killed 150,000 people. Animals run to high.
2004 Cardinal J. Ratzinger, born 1927, Bavaria, becomes Pope Benedict XVI
2005 Hurricane Katrina - Category #5 storm, 10,000 residents in Superdome.
2006 Ted Haggard resigns president of National Association of Evangelicals.
2008 Same sex marriages in Calif. recognized from June thu Nov. in that state.
2008 Obama & Biden - Dem - 365 votes, Mc Cain & Palin, Republicans, 173.
2009 Scientist state that the worst environmental problem is over population.
2010 Thirty three Chilean coal miners trapped underground 69 days, all live.

What after all has maintained the human race on this old globe, despite all the calamities of nature and all the tragic failing of mankind, if not the faith in new possibilities and the courage to address them?
Jane Adams

Supremacy of Human Rights everywhere means freedom. Our support goes to those who struggle to gain rights and keep them.
Dug Hummarskjole, Secretary General,United Nations 1953-1961

The Human Rights Movement throughout the world is producing collective consciousness that will liberate human beings.

To do is to be --- Socrates

To be is to do --- Plato

The way to do is to be. --- Lao-tzu

Age 10 – Six feet off the ground

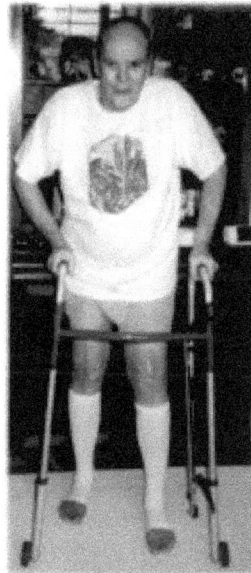

Sixty years later – grounded!

www.ingramcontent.com/pod-product-compliance
Lightning Source LLC
Chambersburg PA
CBHW022114280326
41933CB00007B/377